CUT THE
COST
OF UNI

CUT THE COST OF UNI

How to graduate with less debt

GWENDA THOMAS

trotman | t

Cut the Cost of Uni: How to graduate with less debt

This first edition published in 2012 by Trotman Publishing an imprint of Crimson Publishing, Westminster House, Kew Road, Richmond, TW9 2ND.

© Trotman Publishing, 2012

The right of Gwenda Thomas to be identified as the author of this work has been asserted by her in accordance with the Copyright, Designs and Patents Act, 1988.

Some content in this book was previously published in *Guide to Student Money 2011* © Gwenda Thomas & Trotman Publishing 2009, 2010.

Author: Gwenda Thomas

Cut the Cost of Uni includes information from a survey conducted among students throughout the UK by Trotman Publishing. Every effort has been made to maintain accuracy in providing information and to ensure that this book is as up-to-date as possible. However, changes are constantly taking place in higher education so it is important for readers to check carefully before submitting their applications for funding. The author and publishers cannot be held responsible for any inaccuracies in information supplied to them by third parties or contained in resources and websites listed in the book.

British Library Cataloguing in Publication Data
A catalogue record for this book is available from the British Library.

ISBN 978-1-84455-524-6

Typeset by IDSUK (DataConnection) Ltd
Printed and bound by in the UK by Ashford Colour Press, Gosport, Hants

Contents

Introduction

Why you need this book

The major worry for university students used to be 'will I keep up with my course?' Now it is more likely to be 'can I keep up with the costs?' especially in these times of rising fees and austerity.

Whether you are thinking of going to university or are responsible for someone who is, the headline costs especially in England are frightening. A debt of £50,000, £60,000, even £70,000 when you haven't even started earning is something to be avoided at all costs.

But university doesn't have to cost anything like as much as that.

The fact is you can actually go to university without having any money at all. Surprised? *Cut the Cost of Uni* will tell you how it can be done.

This book has a simple aim, to show you:

► all the different things a student can do to reduce that gargantuan debt
► the most painless ways to cover the debt you are likely to accumulate
► how to make sure you have sufficient money to enjoy studying and benefit from all the opportunities university offers.

And all of this without being too censorious and po-faced about it. Debt isn't a laughing matter, but it doesn't have to be a jail sentence. Even in these times of austerity, there is more to life than worrying over money.

Here are some of the topics covered:

► a breakdown of costs so you know what you are paying for and possible ways to save

- ▶ making sure you benefit from all the freebies: grants, bursaries and scholarships
- ▶ how to cut fees
- ▶ getting a job and getting the most out of it
- ▶ studying abroad in Europe, the US or other places
- ▶ sponsorship in its many forms and guises
- ▶ internships
- ▶ loans and the safe way to borrow money
- ▶ the best kinds of parental help
- ▶ studying in the devolved regions: Scotland, Wales and Northern Ireland
- ▶ courses with cut fees
- ▶ where to find more information
- ▶ comments and budgets from current students
- ▶ studying part time
- ▶ getting a degree without going to university.

The internet is a major source of information if you know what you are looking for. At every twist and turn you will find a list of sites to help develop your knowledge and provide useful back-up information.

Is the current system for undergraduates fair? Should students have to pay such colossal fees?

Cut the Cost of Uni doesn't take sides. We leave that to the comments and quotes from our many student contacts.

The time for arguments is over. *Cut the Cost of Uni* looks at the situation as it is now and sets out to steer you through the funding maze and financial problems. We can't work miracles. But we can smooth out some of the pitfalls and hopefully save you money.

How much will **your** degree cost you? It could be a lot less than you imagined, or even nothing. It could be undertaken in some faraway land or in your own town. We will investigate all possibilities.

While the book is aimed largely at students – after all they do the hard work, pay the bills and have the final burden of debt – parents and teachers have an important role to play too.

Overview

Funding is provided for UK students so they don't need money up front to go to university.

The main source of this funding is **loans**. The maximum fee loan is £9,000 per annum and the maximum maintenance loan is £7,675 per annum.

Loans mean debt.

There is also what we term **debt-free funding**. This doesn't have to be paid back. The maximum maintenance grant is £5,000 per annum and there are university bursaries available, at varying values depending on where you study and your household income.

Other sources of funding include:

► scholarships

► sponsorships

► internships

► work/work experience.

All of these sources of funding will be discussed in the following chapters, along with some more creative and ingenious ways of raising funds to support your studies, and will help objective to *Cut the Cost of Uni* for you.

1 University: what it costs

Take a deep breath. Your maximum debt could be around:

- ► £53,000 for a three-year course
- ► £70,000 for a four-year course.

Monstrous! Impossible! Intolerable!

No student should graduate with that amount of debt! That's what *Cut the Cost of Uni* thinks.

In this chapter we focus mainly on how tuition fees contribute to this overall debt. We give you the facts, right from the start, to chip away at that potential debt, bringing it down, if not to zero, to a more tolerable, more manageable figure.

Spread throughout this chapter are budgets showing what university is costing students today. Remember this is before the great increase in fees.

Where does the money go?

There are a few important facts to get clear in your mind before you make any decisions for or against university.

- ► You don't actually need any money to go to university – not a penny.
- ► Grants, bursaries, loans, even part-time jobs are available to give you enough to pay your fees and to live on while studying.

▶ You are likely to accumulate debt, possibly a massive debt **but** ...

▶ You pay off your debt when you can afford it. Repayments are linked to your earnings, so there will be no rapacious debt collector knocking on the door. If you don't earn, you don't repay.

▶ While at university you need to do everything possible to minimise that debt. *Cut the Cost of Uni* will tell you how.

Even with the help of *Cut the Cost of Uni*, making ends meet at university isn't going to be easy, but it is possible and there should be enough in the kitty to enjoy yourself. So while costs in many universities in the UK have rocketed up, don't let the headline figures scare you off. University is still a great experience – and one not to be missed.

! It's a Fact

This is how the debt stacks up. As a student you will have three main annual costs.

1. Fees: £9,000 maximum.
2. Accommodation: £4,500 approximately.
3. Living expenses: £4,000 approximately (more in London).

Total £17,500 per year.

This is reality. It's the worst-case scenario. Nothing is more painful than staring debt in the face. But, unless you know where the debt comes from, and what you could expect, it is difficult to appreciate the importance of searching out every little cost-saving measure available. In this chapter you will see how your debt can be cut.

Table 1.1. What university costs: Samantha's student budget

Outgoings	Per term
Accommodation	£780
Food	£220
Socialising	£400
Gym	£45
Clothes	£100
Utilities	£60
Books/stationery	£100
Cigarettes	£144
Travel term	£130
Travel home	£40
Total	£2,019 per term
Anticipated final debt	£27,000

Samantha, second year, Psychology, Leeds. Living in rented accommodation, Fees £3,290 per annum. See how Samantha is paying for the cost of university in Chapter 8.

Samantha's Thrift Tip

Sausage meat is a good substitute for mince and much cheaper.

Most of the figures given in this section are based on information taken from university websites and general research undertaken by *Cut the Cost of Uni*, all of which reveals some interesting facts, as you will discover.

Debt and you

Many factors can affect your financial situation. Some students are luckier – or perhaps more determined – than others in:

► raising additional finance
► managing to work as well as study
► choosing to study in cheaper parts of the country

- finding/receiving additional bursary, grants, scholarships, funding
- living at home
- choosing a generous university
- being excellent money managers
- cutting down on going out
- becoming a recluse (not recommended)
- stopping smoking (highly recommended)
- having wealthy parents (luck of the draw)
- coming from a low-income family.

While others:

- find that money slips through their fingers like water
- are great socialisers
- take courses for which they have to travel, buy expensive equipment and books, or include field trips
- have expensive tastes
- have a wide range of hobbies and interests
- study in expensive areas such as London.

Tuition fee facts

As you are probably aware there has been a massive hike in university tuition fees in the UK and this is where the big increase in the cost of university is most painfully felt.

From September 2012, universities can increase fees from just over £3,400 per annum to a maximum of £9,000 per annum. That's a colossal jump. And this is the same for all universities throughout the UK.

However, since devolution, Scotland, Wales and Northern Ireland have gradually introduced many changes to their funding package for students who permanently reside in those regions, especially how much of their tuition fees, if any, they are asked to pay. Full details are given in the section on the devolved regions later in this chapter.

The fee hike is tough especially for English students. In some universities you could be paying almost three times the fees paid by students in previous years. Is it justified? This is how the argument for the hike goes: if we are to maintain the high standards in our universities, and remain competitive, someone has to pay. Sadly, that seems to be the student. Here are the facts.

▶ There will be no help with fees from your local authority or the government in England (while there is in the devolved regions).

▶ Your parents will not be asked to contribute towards fees, though many do.

▶ In general, family income will have no bearing on what you pay.

Not all universities charge the full permitted fee. For example, the list below shows different fees for a bachelor's degree in sociology:

▶ Coventry: £7,500 per annum

▶ Durham: £9,000 per annum

▶ Salford: £8,500 per annum.

Below are some fees for law courses:

▶ Coventry: £7,500 per annum

▶ Greenwich: £8,300 per annum.

▶ Leeds Metropolitan: £8,500 per annum

▶ Manchester: £9,000 per annum.

Will every student pay the same fees?

Unless you come from outside the EU, or are studying in one of the devolved regions, students on the same course at the same university will be charged the same fees. Welsh-domiciled students, however, will have any fees above £3,465 per year paid for by the Welsh Assembly.

There are many universities that charge the same fee for all courses, generally the maximum £9,000. For example:

▶ Cambridge

▶ Durham

...ut there are other universities where course fees within the university vary enormously. Westminster is a good example:

► Journalism: £9,000

► Biochemistry: £8,500

► Law: £8,000

► Economics: £8,000

► Business information systems: £7,500

► *Foundation year courses: £6,000.

(*Note: if this is your second degree you will be charged the full £9,000.)

! It's a fact

Average fees for 2012 across all universities in England is £8,393. Average fees when support from English universities is taken into consideration is £7,793. For more information see Chapter 3.

Source: Complete University Guide

Universities and also students have argued that by charging less than the maximum fee the university will be rated as a second-class university. True or false? You must make your own judgement. And pay the price.

As you can see **fees** are something of a minefield. Picking a course or indeed a university isn't easy these days.

👍 top tip

Cut your debt: make the right choices before you apply.

Obviously, you should not pick your course of study only on the basis of the cheapness of the course but it helps to know the possible savings.

Table 1.2. Cut the cost of uni: study a cheaper subject

Outgoings p.a.	Journalism course	Business information systems course
Fees	£9,000	£7,500
Accommodation	£4,500	£4,500
Living expenses	£4,000	£4,000
Total	£17,500	£16,000
	Saving p.a.	£1,500

We haven't looked into the content of any of the example courses here; that is your job as the future student. University websites offer plenty of detail on their courses and make sure you talk to departmental staff. Despite the need to cut your costs (and that is the aim of this book) we must stress that it is even more important to make sure you are studying the right course for you. Course drop-out figures are escalating. Over 30,000 students dropped out of their university courses in the UK last year, a record number. If the more expensive course turns out to be the best option for you, you'll need to look at other ways of saving money.

Knowledge is a cost saver. Do your research and make sure you make the right decisions.

Make sure you are up to date

Funding for university in the UK changes annually. The information in this edition of *Cut the Cost of Uni* is based on university funding for the year 2012–13. Make sure you have the right information for the year when you are starting your degree course. Changes are rarely retrospective so once you have started your studies it is unlikely that the costs will change fundamentally for the duration of your course.

Who pays the fees?

Students are responsible for ensuring their fees are paid. Although this does not mean that as a student you must produce the cash, it does mean you must organise how they are to be paid.

You can take out a tution fee loan with the Student Loans Company (SLC) which will pay them for you (see Chapter 8), or your parents could pay your fees. If you are not taking out a loan to cover your fees, or only a partial loan, you must let your college or university know and agree to the payment arrangements.

Where could the money come from?

- ▶ Grants and bursaries (see Chapter 4).
- ▶ Sponsorship (see Chapter 5).
- ▶ Ingenuity and hard work (see Chapters 6 and 7).
- ▶ Parents: there is nothing to stop parents/family paying fees.
- ▶ Last resort: student fee loan (see Chapter 8).

University help with fees

Universities can charge what they like for a course (up to the maximum of £9,000 per annum) and what they ask is what you must pay.

However, all universities charging over £6,000 for fees must provide some support to disadvantaged students, i.e. students from low-income families. The family income must be under £25,000 to receive full support. The support could take the form of:

- ▶ a fee waiver
- ▶ accommodation discount
- ▶ a bursary
- ▶ a scholarship.

For full details of debt-free funding see Chapter 4.

! It's a Fact

The hike in fees is not retrospective. Students who started their degree course before 2012 will stick with the old fee arrangement for the rest of their course.

Will tuition fees increase?

Tution fees of £9,000 aren't the end of the story of course. Fees do and will go up. Ever since fees for students were introduced they have increased every year at least in line with inflation, and there is no reason to think this will change. However, it is unlikely that this year's massive hike will be repeated anytime soon.

What students say about fees

'£9,000 and you only get two days' teaching.'

First year, LPC, UWE

'It's a crazy amount of money and we still have to buy everything else.'
Second year, Museum and Gallery Studies, St Andrews

'The hike in tuition fees is forcing us to value an education which I see as invaluable while cutting a clear line between those who can and cannot pay.'
Third year, Politics, Cambridge

Cash saver for parents

If parents want to pay for your fees but will have to borrow to do so, it's worth remembering that the student fee loan is probably still the cheapest money you can borrow. It is only available to students. However, you might be able to come to a cost-saving family arrangement so parents pay off your debts once you graduate (see Chapter 8).

Dropping out

If you drop out of your course you will have to pay off your fee debt (if you have one) for all the completed years and possibly for the year or part of the year you are currently in. So it's not a cheap way out.

Typical drop-out debt figures to pay:

- ▶ 25% of fees for the first term
- ▶ 50% of fees for the second term
- ▶ 100% of fees for the third term.

You will probably have a maintenance bill to pay back as well. If you realise your course mistake before 1 December in your first year you may get away with paying no fees since this is the date when the universities are paid by the SLC. But don't bank on it. The best advice is to make a decision and tell your course director as soon as possible.

 top tip

Cut your debt: don't be a £9,000 drop out – speak up and make a move.

Changing course

If you want to change your course you will need to discuss your fee arrangement with your university. If you are changing to another course in the same university, fees may not be a problem, but if you are moving to another university it might be more difficult and more costly.

Students can let the SLC know of their decision to change course by logging onto their online account and using the change of circumstances facility.

i **advice note**

Don't pick a course on price; dropping out of university can be costly and you'll have nothing to show for it (see page 13).

Devolutionary differences

The three devolved regions of the UK are offering their own students a better deal regarding fees.

Scotland

You pay no tuition fees for your university education, and because of EU regulations this also applies to non–UK EU students. But be warned, step over the border to study and you'll face the full force of the fee bill up to £9,000.

Students from the rest of the UK who study in Scotland do pay fees and most universities will ask for the maximum £9,000 per annum. Universities have come up with some cunning ideas to lessen the debt burden for other UK students and so encourage them to study in Scotland. These include the following.

▸ Fees for a full four-year course capped at £27,000. Bachelor's degrees in Scotland are generally four years. This means you get a four-year course for the price of three years.

▸ Three-year course: students join the course in the second year so you only study and pay for three years.

▸ Help with fees for low-income families with fee waivers (see Chapter 4).

Scottish students attending universities in England, Wales and Northern Ireland pay the full fees demanded by the university.

Table 1.3. Cut the cost of uni: If you're a Scottish student, live and study in Scotland

Outgoings	England	Scotland
Fees	£9,000	£0
Accommodation	£4,500	£4,500
Living expenses	£4,000	£4,000
Total	£17,500	£8,500
	Saving p.a.	£9,000

! It's a Fact

No tuition fee debt is the big plus if you live and study in Scotland.

Wales

Welsh domiciled students pay fees of just £3,465 wherever they study in the UK. The Welsh Government then picks up the rest of the fee cost up to £9,000 per annum.

Students from all other parts of the UK attending Welsh universities will pay the full university fee, generally £9,000 per annum. Bursaries for students from low-income families are available from some universities in Wales (see Chapter 4).

Table 1.4. Cut the cost of uni: If you're a Welsh student, study where you like in the UK

Outgoings	English students	Welsh students
Fees	£9,000	£3,465
Accommodation	£4,500	£4,500
Living expenses	£4,000	£4,000
Total	£17,500	£11,965
	Saving p.a.	£5,535

! It's a Fact

Students who live in Wales have the widest choice of fee savings since they can study anywhere in the UK for a bargain price.

Northern Ireland

Students who live and study in Northern Ireland pay fees of £3,465 per annum. If they study at a UK university outside Northern Ireland they pay the same fees as the rest of the UK: up to £9,000 per annum.

Students from the rest of the UK who decide to study in Northern Ireland pay fees of up to £9,000 per annum.

If you are studying in **the Republic of Ireland,** there are no fees to pay, just a registration fee of €2,250 which for Northern Ireland students will be paid by the Northern Ireland Department for Employment and Learning.

Table 1.5. Cut the cost of uni: If you're a Northern Irish student, live in Northern Ireland

Outgoings	Study in England	Study in Northern Ireland
Fees	£9,000	£3,465
Accommodation	£4,500	£4,500
Living expenses	£4,000	£4,000
Total	£17,500	£11,965
	Saving p.a.	£5,535

Fees for part-time students

These will depend on the intensity of the course you take.

▶ England: up to £6,750 per annum for a full course (see Chapter 6 for full details).

▶ Scotland domiciled students: fees vary between £0 and £1,820 for home students.

▶ Wales: unregulated – set by the individual institution.

▶ Northern Ireland: unregulated – set by the individual institution.

For further information about fees

Students in England

▶ Student Finance 'matters to me' factsheets: www.direct.gov.uk/studentfinance
▶ Student Finance Hotline: 0845 300 5090 (textphone: 0845 604 4434)
▶ Student Finance 'how to' videos: www.direct.gov.uk/sfvideos

- Student Finance Zone at The Student Room: www.thestudentroom.co.uk/studentfinance
- For a quick read, try 20 key facts at www.moneysavingexpert.com/students
- BIS Department for Business Innovation & Skills www.bis.gov.uk/studentfinance
- Money4MedStudents: www.money4medstudents.org/506

Students in Scotland

- Student Awards Agency for Scotland: www.saas.gov.uk
- General queries: 0300 555 0505
- Post: SAAS, Gyleview House, 3 Redheughs Rigg, Edinburgh, EH12 9HH
- The Scottish Government: www.scotland.gov.uk (key in 'financial help for students')

Students in Wales

- Student Finance Wales: www.studentfinancewales.co.uk
- Tel: 0845 602 8845

Students in Northern Ireland

- www.direct.gov.uk/en/Nl1/Newsroom/index.htm
- www.studentfinanceeni.co.uk
- Department for Employment and Learning (Northern Ireland), Rathgael House, Balloo Road, Bangor, Co. Down BT19 7PR or tel: 028 9025 7710 or visit the website: www.delni.gov.uk.

Looking across the channel

Would studying in Europe be cheaper?

Compared with the rest of Europe, our fees are high – very high indeed. In fact in some EU countries you pay no fees at all. So you would certainly make a colossal saving on fees by looking across the channel to further your education.

In this current climate, the US is also looking like a more attractive proposition especially for fully funded students and those from low-income families as many universities in the US offer generous funding packages.

Studying abroad is a radical step and fees are just one aspect to be considered. Unless time spent in an EU country is part of your degree, you would be outside the UK funding system – so there would be no grants, bursaries or loans from the UK government to back you up while you studied for your degree. Any fees would need to be paid up front and the rest would be 'pay as you go'. And that could be where the problem lies. On the plus side: you would not be stacking up an enormous debt. On the minus side: how do you actually pay your way in a foreign country?

If you have access to funds and you are anticipating paying your way, then Europe could be a cheaper option. But there are ways and means of getting help if you start digging and are determined. More details can be found in the section on studying abroad in Chapter 3.

! It's a Fact

Not a linguist? Many European universities offer courses taught in English. See Chapter 3 for more details.

Courses with different fee structures

Industrial placements

Students who spend an entire year of a course on an industrial placement at home or abroad will pay reduced fees and they will also probably be paid a salary too. Universities in England can set their own reduced fee figure, to a maximum of around 50% of the current fee. If you are on a thin sandwich course (where placements are usually between two and six months) or the placement is for less than a full year, full fees will probably be charged.

But why, you might ask, do you have to pay fees when you are not enjoying the advantages of university? This is said to be a contribution towards the cost to the institution of administrative and pastoral arrangements relating to the placement. For more details on industrial placements and how they can help cut your debt see Chapter 7.

Foundation courses

Some courses include a preliminary or foundation year. These are designed to prepare students for study in their chosen subject if their qualifications or experience are not sufficient to start a degree-level course of study. The same financial support is available to students on a foundation year as for undergraduates, providing – and this is crucial – the following conditions are met:

► the foundation year is an integral part of the course

► the course as a whole is eligible for student support

► you enrol for the whole course and not just the foundation year.

The following shows examples of how foundation fees can vary.

► The University of Westminster charges £6,000 for all its foundation courses.

► Leeds University foundation fees are on a sliding scale based on family income. With a family income of £25,000 or below you pay nothing; for an income of £25,000–£42,600 you pay £4,500; and with a family income of £42,601 and above you pay the full course fees of £9,000.

Students from abroad

EU students

EU students will be treated on a similar basis to their UK counterparts regarding fees. This means they will pay:

► no fees if studying in Scotland

► £3,465 per annum if studying in Wales

► £3,465 per annum if studying in Northern Ireland

► £9,000 per annum max if studying in England. The actual amount will depend on the fee being charged at the university of choice.

i **advice note**

For more information on tuition fees for EU students contact: Student Finance Services European Team, PO Box 89, Darlington DL1 9AZ. Helpline tel: +44 (0)141 243 3570 (Monday to Friday 9a.m.– 5.30p.m.), website: www.direct.gov.uk/studentfinance.

Non-EU students

Even though most UK students pay fees, the full cost of a course is subsidised by the government. Students from countries outside the EU will be charged the full cost of the course and can legally be charged higher tuition fees than UK students – so for a first degree you can think in terms of £14,000–£16,000 per annum. It could be up to £21,000 or even £31,000 for medicine or a veterinary course. Full fees are paid in all regions of the UK.

2 Your living expenses

You've seen what you can expect to pay in university fees but these aren't the only costs you will face while you are at university. You also need somewhere to live and will need to pay for food and equipment for your course. In this chapter we will consider all other expenses such as:

► accommodation
► living costs
► travel
► socialising
► all the little extras: insurance, books and field trips.

Living expenses have to be paid for largely by you. And they are not cheap. Maintenance grants and bursaries are available to UK students largely from low-income families (see Chapter 4 for full details). Loans are also available.

Wherever your money comes from, managing it is your responsibility and it's not going to be easy. It's you who will have to eke it out and decide whether you eat, heat or go to the ball. You will need to make sure you can finance your accommodation costs, travel expenses, food bills, and still have enough for books, equipment, and importantly, having a good time.

There is little doubt, living at home is the best way to make a significant saving in your living expenses. If your parents don't ask you to pay rent or for food the saving could be well over £3,000 per annum.

How much will I need?

This is what some universities are currently suggesting you'll need to cover your accommodation and all your living expenses for an academic year (take these figures as a rough guide):

▶ Cardiff: £6,480 per annum

▶ Edinburgh: £7,000 per annum

▶ Exeter: £8,500 per annum

▶ King's College London: £11,197 per annum

▶ Manchester: £8,240 per annum

▶ Newcastle: £7,700 per annum

▶ Queen's Belfast: £7,500 per annum

▶ Average: £7,570 per annum (£11,197 per annum in London).

Accommodation

Accommodation will probably account for half of your living costs. If it's full board in university accommodation, you are looking at over three-quarters of your total outgoing expenses.

Finding the right place to live is important, especially in your first year. It can affect your whole attitude to your institution, your course, the town or city where you are staying, making the right friends and whether you actually do well. If it's half an hour's walk or a bus ride across town to get to the library, you may think twice about going there. If you're stuck in a bedsit with a grumpy landlord and no other students around you, the weekends could be very long and lonely. Halls are generally thought to be the best option for first years, but they aren't right for everyone.

'It is impossible to get a decent night's sleep because of noisy students returning after a night out.'

First year, Arts, Robert Gordon University

> 'Occasionally you'll hear people running along the corridor at 2a.m. But
> mostly people are considerate.'
>
> Modern Languages, Cambridge

Most institutions give first-year students first refusal on halls of residence and most students jump at the chance. We'd agree with this even if it's not the cheapest option. It gives you a circle of ready-made friends and a great social life. But for some students, living with a hundred or so other people, sharing bathrooms, meal times, TV programmes, problems, passions – even bedrooms – can mean unbearable strain. Others thrive on the camaraderie. You will need to weigh up the pros and cons and decide whether halls is the best option for you.

Finding accommodation

Institution prospectuses will generally give you information about halls of residence, though these may not be altogether bias-free. The accommodation sections on university websites are generally very good with plenty of photos of what to expect.

Contact your students' union, they may also have a view – ask if they have an alternative prospectus or students' union handbook.

☑ **what you need to know when looking for accommodation**

- ▶ Cost
- ▶ Whether rooms are shared
- ▶ Eating arrangements: full board, half board, kitchen/self-catered
- ▶ Number of students sharing facilities
- ▶ Facilities provided (e.g. laundry facilities)
- ▶ Some establishments offer accommodation other than the norm, such as en-suite, up-to-the minute facilities or an out-of-town location
- ▶ Distance from college or campus
- ▶ Distance from library
- ▶ Distance from centre of town
- ▶ Shops

- ▶ Transport availability: frequency and cost
- ▶ Last bus home
- ▶ Facilities in location
- ▶ Parking

The institution accommodation office is responsible for placing students in halls of residence and will send you details once you've accepted a place. It will also help you to find rented accommodation.

If it has to be accommodation in the private sector, ask for the university-approved accommodation list. Above all, check out the accommodation for yourself if possible.

☑ check what's included in the rent

- ▶ The number of meals per day
- ▶ The number of days per week that meals are served
- ▶ The number of weeks in the academic year
- ▶ Are you paying for vacations (if it is not university accommodation)?
- ▶ Utilities: gas, electricity and water
- ▶ Insurance
- ▶ Internet connection
- ▶ TV

Cut the Cost of Uni asked students how they decided on their accommodation and whether they would recommend that method. It would seem there are four main ways for students to find accommodation: the university itself, the internet, letting agencies and word of mouth.

By far the most popular way of finding accommodation is through your university website, especially in your first year. Most students found this very satisfactory. The second most favoured option was the internet, while letting agencies were also popular. In some places there are also accommodation fairs, which offer a wide range of choice. Try and visit the accommodation when you visit your university.

What students say: how to save on accommodation

'Catered halls is much cheaper. £2 at most for an evening meal.'
Third year, Geography, Royal Holloway (rent £1,650 per term)

'Having bills included in rent has saved us money and means we don't worry about turning the heating up.'
Second year, Natural Science, Durham (rent £1,387 per term)

'I saved £1,000 by sharing a room. It wasn't as bad as I thought. We didn't argue. In fact the other girl never spoke to me the whole time. Amazing! So we never fell out. It was like having a single room.'
First year, Drama & Theatre Studies, Royal Holloway

Costs vary significantly between different types of accommodation and different universities. Whether you want en-suite or are prepared to share; whether it's self-catering or meals included. Much higher costs can be expected in the London colleges in particular.

! It's a Fact

The estimated costs for living in halls of residence is between £78 per week and £150 per week.

No-frills accommodation

If you can do without all the extra mod cons you can save yourself around £30 a week – but it does mean a bog standard room with shared bathrooms, toilets and cooking facilities and this could be with up to 12 fellow students.

Typical accommodation costs

Manchester University has the largest number of accommodation places for students of any university with over 9,200 places in 29 different buildings all offering something different. Typical examples are given below.

Self-catering:

► Bog standard no basin £79 per week.
► Single en-suite £118 per week.
► Deluxe en-suite £121 per week.

Catered:

► Basic no basin £81 per week.
► En-suite with shower £121 per week.
► Super single £150 per week.

For a list of things to ask and check when choosing accommodation see page 25.

Table 2.1. Cut the cost of uni: with no frills accommodation

Outgoings p.a.	Deluxe	Bog standard
Accommodation*	£4,598 p.a. (£121 p.w.)	£3,002 p.a. (£79 p.w.)
Living expenses	£4,000	£4,000
Total	£8,598	£7,002
	Saving p.a.	£1,596

*Based on a 38 week academic year

What students say: how to save money on campus
'I went for shared toilets and showers and was saving £40 a week.'
First year, Primary Teaching, Stranmillis University College
(rent £98 per week)

'Although en-suite is preferred, it is an unnecessary expense.'
First year, Law, Sussex (rent £96 per week)

---

cash crisis

Students in the South East but studying outside the London area are thought to be suffering particularly badly, as they are being asked to pay London-equivalent rents while not qualifying for the larger student loans available to students who study in the capital.

Privately rented accommodation

This may not vary significantly in cost from university accommodation. If it's a long way from your campus it could be much cheaper. The most important aspect is what it includes.

☑ **things to check**

- ► Are gas, electricity and water included the rent? Probably not.
- ► The landlord's insurance.
- ► Will you need to pay a deposit up front to secure the tenancy? (Often at least a month's rent, possibly more.)
- ► Try and talk to previous tenants and see what the landlord is like.

Check out the length and terms of your accommodation contract. A recent survey of university students found that more and more landlords were asking students to sign 52-week contracts for accommodation. This means you are paying rent during the vacations when you are not there. Try and negotiate this down to 11 months at least.

'Private accommodation is a lot cheaper: £90 per week on campus, private £60 per week.'

Fifth year, Architecture, Dundee

'Accommodation further from uni was £400 cheaper a year.'
First year, Biomedical Science, Dundee (rent £1,550 per term)

Table 2.2. What university costs: Rachel's student budget

Outgoings per term	
Accommodation	£1,330
Food	£120
Socialising	£120
Mobile phone	£120
Clothes	£90
Petrol	£360
Total	£2,140
Fees	£3,375
Anticipated final debt	£14,000

Rachel, first year, BEd Primary Education, Stranmillis University College Belfast. In halls, fully catered. See how Rachel is paying for her university course in Chapter 8.

Rachel's Thrift Tip

Save money: *find someone to share your car when driving home.*

💣 cash crisis for medics

Medical students who have to undertake a placement away from their university may find they are paying for somewhere to live on that placement for a couple of months while still paying for the accommodation in their university town.

Don't forget you will also probably have to pay utility bills (gas, water, electricity etc.) if you are in private rented accommodation but you probably won't be responsible for these costs in university accommodation.

Utilities (gas, electricity, water, internet)

What universities advise:

- ► University of Birmingham estimates £8 per week
- ► Newcastle University estimates £15 per week
- ► London South Bank University comes in at around £10 per week

Cut the Cost of Uni says be vigilant, nothing is going up faster right now than gas and electricity.

What students say: how to save money on your bills

'We paid our landlord in bulk months in advance in order to receive a minor discount – every little helps!'

Second year, History and Education, Keele

'We had the option of paying an extra £10 a week each to cover bills but decided not to take it. There was more hassle, but we saved £200 each. We also got a better and cheaper internet provider.'

Third year, Maths, Durham

---

 cash crisis

Your deposit will be kept against loss or damage until you vacate the premises. But what if your landlord won't give back your deposit when you move out? For students in England or Wales check www.direct.gov.uk/en/HomeAndCommunity/Privaterenting/Tenancies/DG_189120 and make sure your Landlord is adhering to the new law. Of course, if you trash the place, you can't expect to see your money back – it works both ways.

Similar legislation is on the way in Scotland, and in Northern Ireland a scheme called Building Sound Foundations is on the way.

To give you some more ideas about where to live, and the costs involved, we asked students what they thought. Here are their stories.

How to cut your debt by living in halls: Robert's story

Robert is a third-year Geography student at Royal Holloway College. He is back in university accommodation after spending the previous year in a shared house. He decided on halls for his final year because he thought it would be cheaper and much less hassle than catering for himself. He was right.

Last year's rent plus food was around £6,000. This year it will be more like £4,500. Says Robert, 'I probably ate better and more healthily when catering for myself, but time is a priority right now.

'The food is a little like school dinners, but adequate and highly subsidised. At around £2 a main course (often variations on pasta dishes), and another £1 for a sweet if you need it, you can't complain.'

Payment is through your university card, which also doubles as your room key and library ticket.

Robert has a sizeable en-suite room, in a block that caters just for third and fourth years. He says 'It is quiet which is essential for serious study.' (Unlike in his first year when he was on a corridor with 12 freshers sharing washing and cooking facilities, socialising together and coming home late.)

Halls are friendly: 'There are five of us who generally go down to the dining room and eat together.

'Our block is on campus and everything is within walking distance – the gym, the dining room, the library, lecture halls, bars, club rooms.'

Robert's friends from rock climbing and ski and snowboarding are at the centre of his socialising. 'I never spend more than £5 a week.'

Sharing a flat: Shona's story

Shona is a third-year Anatomical Science student at Dundee University. She lives with four other girls in a privately rented flat. It is spacious but fairly rudimentary. 'Everything is there', she says, 'but there's nothing fancy. The walls are breeze blocks; there is only one bathroom and no bath.

'We were worried at first, one shower, five girls, four of whom dye their hair. But there is never a queue.

'It's off campus, but very convenient: my lecture halls are opposite, my favourite bar behind and it's a great party venue. And as we are all coming up for 21 there are plenty of them. We buy the plastic glasses, and everybody comes with booze.

'We eat together when we can, it's always cheaper. Some student houses shop and eat together all the time and that is a great saving, but it's difficult when you all have different timetables. If we are all in on Sunday, I'll do a roast.'

Shona's rent is £240 a month. 'I spend another £400 on food, socialising, downloads, cocktails, beauty products and everything else. We have set up a bank account into which we pay £30 a month each to cover bills and a kitty for household products.

'I like living off campus, I feel more independent, negotiating with estate agents, chasing mail, dealing with bills, feeding myself, and looking after my own finances.'

Other accommodation costs

Council tax

Students are largely exempt from paying council tax. Certainly, if you live in a hall of residence, college accommodation, a student house or somewhere in which all the residents are students, you will be exempt. If you live in a house where there are already two adults, your presence does not add to the bill. If you live in a house with one adult, that person will not lose their 25% single occupancy discount providing they can supply proof that you are a student.

However, you may just find you have to pay up. For example:

► a full-time student moves into a house shared with non-students and the housemates expect them to contribute to the council tax bill

► a flatmate drops out of their course during the summer and fails to claim benefit

► a part-time student thought they would be exempt but they are not

► a postgraduate student is writing up work and is refused student status by local authorities.

If in doubt, go to your university welfare officer – they are usually on the ball.

What students say: how to save money on accommodation
'We negotiated a guarantee that our rent wouldn't change for two years.'
Third year, Psychology, Dundee (rent £1,475 per term)
'Live at home.'   Second year, Health and Leisure,
Stranmillis University College (rent zero)

Insurance

Do you really need it? If not, could this be a good place to start cutting costs? *Cut the Cost of Uni* doesn't think so. At least be careful.

What's my stuff worth?

This may surprise you! A recent survey completed by Endsleigh, specialists in student insurance, and the NUS shows that, on average, this tech-savvy generation of students take nearly £3,000 worth of belongings to university, and this is not going unnoticed by thieves. These possessions are often highly valuable and portable – for example laptops, iPods, iPads, iPhones, tablets, MP3 players, digital cameras and games consoles.

Students regularly have an average of £1,165 worth of gadgets on them and that doesn't include jewellery, cash and credit cards. You are a walking temptation. Ask yourself, what would you do if you lost the lot?

Insurance is another drain on your resources, but it could be money well spent and save a lot of heartache.

Table 2.3. Which of these do you own?

	Estimated value
PC	£660
Laptop	£636
Tablet	£329
MP3 player	£77
iPhone	£363
Stereo equipment	£135
Digital camera	£191
Television	£238
Musical instrument	£684
Sports equipment	£208
DVDs	£156
CDs	£132
Kitchen stuff	£111
Bicycle	£262
Downloads	Incalculable: backup essential

With all types of insurance, costs vary depending on what you choose to cover. Read the small print: what looks like a cheap deal doesn't always end up that way. Many include an excess figure (the amount you must pay towards a claim).

Family insurance

Start with your parents' insurance – if the family insurance already covers you then this is obviously your cheapest option. Make sure it covers your possessions out of the house.

But is it the best buy for parents? A recent survey discovered the following.

- Students are 60% more likely to make a claim.
- Any claim will affect the parents' no claims bonus discount and so increase their premium.

Survey carried out by Endsleigh Insurance 2011.

***i* advice note**

You can also take out insurance to cover the fees you have paid just in case you are ill and can't complete your course.

University policy

If you are living in halls, you may find there is a comprehensive policy covering all students and that this is included in your rent bill. If you are living in rented accommodation, the landlord of the house or flat you rent should have the premises covered by insurance for fire and structural damage, but this is unlikely to cover your personal possessions.

Open house to thieves

Students tend to keep open house, and because people are coming and going all the time security is often lax. If you can leave stuff at home do. If you do have a lot of expensive possessions at university it might be worthwhile considering taking out your own insurance, especially if you carry expensive belongings around. Rates for personal insurance depend on where you live. It costs more if you live in a big city than a sleepy rural town. In a crime hotspot, rates can be prohibitive.

Insurance: best buy

Most of the banks offer student cover. All are different and should be compared along with companies such as Endsleigh, which are specialists in student insurance.

Typical example: NatWest's Essential Contents Insurance is ideal
for the student living in rented accommodation because it offers
a 'pick and mix' cover for the things that are valuable to you, such
as laptops, iPods and mobile phones, which means that you don't
pay for cover you don't need. It can include cover for walk-in theft
(though not for money).

Insuring your bike

You might think a bike is easy to insure. But any student intending to
take a bicycle to university must think in terms of having it pinched,
or at least relocated without permission. Insurance companies
certainly think that way. Here are a few tips.

▶ A good padlock and detachable wheel or saddle should be your first form
of insurance.

▶ Consider exchanging that expensive mountain bike for something that
looks as if it's come off the tip.

▶ Typical insurance cover for bikes worth up to £400 against accidental
damage and theft anywhere in the UK costs around £40 a year.

Table 2.4. **What university costs:** Henry's student budget

Outgoings per term	
Accommodation	£1,700
Food	£150
Socialising (mostly alcohol)	£500
Clothes	£70
Books	£60
Events	£40
Mobile	£70
Travel (term)	£20
Travel (home)	£100
Total	£2,710 per term
Fees	£3,445
Anticipated final debt	£9,000

Henry, first year, Classics, Durham. Living in college accommodation.

Henry's Thrift Tip

Save money: *walk home in a group or share a taxi.*

Eating, drinking, shopping and other living expenses

While your accommodation will probably take at least half of your available resources, how will you spend the rest?

Estimated costs in this section are from universities around the country and can be found on their websites; or come from *Cut the Cost of Uni*'s student experience research.

Food

Once you have a roof over your head, your next major expense will be food:

▶ eating in is always cheaper

▶ eating together is cheaper still and probably more nutritious.

▶ crisps, drinks and coffee at university snack bars can be expensive – try tap water

▶ take a packed lunch.

Your weekly food bill: what universities suggest

▶ University of Newcastle: £37.50 per week.

▶ London South Bank University: main meals £50–£60 per week, plus lunches and snacks £25 per week.

▶ University of Oxford: £56 per week.

Your weekly food bill: what students say

The biggest eater *Cut the Cost of Uni* found was in Dundee with a food bill of £79 per week. The most frugal eater was also in Dundee, spending just £10 per week.

The average weekly shopping basket was around £28.

What students say: tips for saving on your shopping

'Never go shopping when hungry – it will lead to impulse buying.'
First year, Business Management, Sussex

'Beards are not only fashionable and cool but help you save on shaving foam and razors.'
First year, Psychology, York St John

'Write a shopping list and stick to it.'
Second year, American Studies and History, Keele

'Go to Tesco after 2p.m. and raid the reduced section.'
Fourth year, Illustration, Jordanstone College of Art

When to shop

The student who gave us the final shopping tip above was on to something, as *Cut the Cost of Uni* discovered when they started to make enquiries.

Most supermarkets have regular times when they reduce the prices of products that are coming up to their sell-by date. To get the best bargains you need to know which supermarkets cut what, when and by how much. Here we pass on to you what we discovered.

Table 2.5. Supermarket discount times

Store	Reductions			
Tesco	12 noon 25%	5p.m. 50%	8p.m. 75%	9p.m. 80% (if anything left)
Sainsbury's	10a.m.–midday	Best bargains from 5p.m. onwards		
ASDA	Bakery from 12 noon	Best bargains from 5p.m.		
Co-op	8a.m. 25%	3p.m.–5p.m. 50%	Later 75%	

39

Your local supermarket may have a slightly different cost cutting timetable. Find a friendly assistant and find out when is the best time to raid the reduced counter to eat now or put in the freezer. Happy eating!

Cut the cost of socialising: stay in and save £25 a night.

Socialising/entertainment
What students spend on socialising
The top social activities for students include clubbing, pubbing, gigs, cinema and drinking. Universities estimate that the following is spent by their students on socialising/entertainment.

▶ Birmingham: £50 per week.

▶ Bristol: £40 per week (approximately £1,531 per annum).

▶ Cardiff: £26 per week (approximately £990 per annum).

▶ City University London: £20–£50 per week.

▶ Exeter: £35 per week (£1,085 per annum).

▶ Kent: £25–£55 per week (£975–£2,145 per annum).

▶ Oxford: £28 per week (approximately £780 per annum).

▶ Sheffield: £17.15 per week (approximately £652 per annum).

What students told *Cut the Cost of Uni*
The biggest spender came in at £600 per term (second-year student, Early Childhood Studies, Stranmillis University College). While the most frugal, stay-at-home student spent £30 per term (first-year student, Biomedical Sciences, Dundee University). General expenditure was between £200 and £400 per term.

Up to £25 was regularly spent on alcohol on a night out. As for cigarettes, only 10% of students said they smoked, with an average bill of £12.97 per week.

What students say: save on socialising
'Pre-load (drink before you go out).'

'Make every other drink water.'

'Take a hip flask, just make sure you avoid the bouncers.'

'Entertain at home.'

'Only go out on student nights and go out early.'

Table 2.6. **What university costs:** Jessica's student budget

Outgoings per term	
Accommodation	£1,800
Food	£100
Socialising	£300
Clothes	£100
Books	£100
Travel (term)	£80
Travel (home)	£70
Total	£2,550 per term
Fees	£3,000
Anticipated final debt	£15,000

Jessica, third year, BSc Maths, Durham. Lives in college accommodation.

Jessica's Thrift Tip

Save money: *cut the chips and pizza on the way home after a night out and eat at home.*

Course costs: books, course materials, etc.

The cost of course materials depends on what subject you are studying. If you are on a fine arts course then materials are going to be your most expensive item, if you are studying law then it is likely to be books. Figures given here are only a guide. Students generally spent more on books and course materials in the autumn term and in their first year than at any other time.

What universities suggest:

▶ Cardiff: £315 per annum

▶ Exeter: £300 per annum

▶ Kent: £390–£585 per annum

▶ Newcastle: £405 per annum

▶ Oxford: £290 per annum

▶ Sheffield: £229 per annum

▶ London South Bank University: £150–£250 per annum.

Some courses that are likely to have significant additional costs for books, equipment and field trips are mathematical sciences and computer science, medicine, dentistry and education. There will be others, so do your research before you apply.

What students say: save money on your course books

'Check out your institution library. Is it well stocked with books on your subject? Is it close to where you live?'

'eBooks may be cheaper and easier to handle.'

'Don't buy books before you go to university, you may not need them all.'

'Buy second-hand if you can. New books are very expensive.'

'Your university or college may have a second-hand bookshop.'

'Try the internet – there are many sites for buying and selling textbooks.'

'Search the internet for 'legal' downloads.'

'Try Amazon or eBay; Abebooks (www.abebooks.co.uk) is excellent for technical books.'

'Go halves with a course mate.'

'Sell books when you've finished your course, even second-hand ones, and get your money back.'

Field trips
Many courses include field trips: geography, biology, astrophysics, computer science, music, sustainable development, medicine, education, ancient and medieval history, geology – the list goes on. And many of these trips are mandatory. Contact the university department and ask what field trips are included, and the likely costs and if they are mandatory before you make your application.

Photocopying, library costs and fines, etc.
Many universities provide a photocopying card, which can ease your costs. For those on courses where study covers topics in a wide range of books, the cost can be considerable. Many of our student contacts said most of their copying costs went on ink and paper for their own printers.

Mobile phones

Most students today have a mobile, so you have an idea of the monthly cost. If your parents are currently paying for this, check whether they are going to continue to foot the bill. New deals have brought bills down and many cover the cost of calls. It is worth keeping your eye on the market. Most students rely on their mobiles and some don't ever bother with a landline.

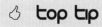 **top tip**

Cut your debt: with a £10 per month mobile deal.

Students are telling us that their monthly mobile bills are somewhere between £25 and £40. Always compare contracts.

As a brief guide we looked at SIM card deals only:

- 3sim: 300 minutes + 3000 texts + 1GB = £10 per month
- Vodafone: 300 minutes + unlimited texts = £8 per month
- Orange: 150 minutes + 500 texts + 250MB = £7 per month.

Source: uswitch.com

Insurance is an added expense to consider but ask yourself the following:

- could you live without your phone?
- would your whole social life collapse if it went missing?

Remember insurance is especially important in the student environment where things have a tendency to go missing.

Typical costs of straight mobile phone insurance.

- Accidental damage and overseas cover costs around £3.99 per month.
- Add theft and unauthorised calls for £5.99 per month.
- Add loss for £6.99 per month.

Internet

It would seem this is no longer a major expense for students. Many find it is included in their rent. A broadband connection can mean a monthly bill of as little as £5 shared amongst all the housemates, but the cheapest isn't necessarily the best. Make sure you have enough speed and the download limit will be enough to accommodate everybody's needs. Look for the special offers, and if you are hoping to hop from one offer to another make sure there are no tie-in clauses in the contract and you are not still paying for the internet when you have left your lodgings.

Cut your debt: become a charity shop junkie.

Clothing

With universities estimating annual bills of £270–£595 the cost does not seem excessive. Around £300 was the annual spend that most students gave to *Cut the Cost of Uni*. But clothes are a very personal thing, some see them as an essential while others regard them as a luxury. Only you will know if you are a secret retail shopaholic.

What universities estimate students spend on clothing:

- ▶ Birmingham £570 per annum
- ▶ Bristol £595 per annum
- ▶ Cardiff £270 per annum
- ▶ Exeter £270 per annum
- ▶ Kent £390 per annum
- ▶ Manchester £375 per annum
- ▶ Oxford £430 per annum
- ▶ Sheffield £429 per annum.

What students said they spend on clothing

First-year students seem to spend less, possibly because they come from home well equipped. Some said just £20–£25 a term. The average figure was £87 per term for first-years.

Second-years and above tend to spend more but not extravagantly so. The highest figure we found was £400 per term, while the average figure was £165 per term.

Thrift Tips

Save money on your clothes

► Ask for clothes/a voucher for presents.

► Check out the local charity shops.

► Last year's jeans make good shorts.

► Share with your housemates where you can.

► Learn to sew and make a bit on the side sewing for others.

► Shop on eBay: great bargains providing you set a limit and stick to it.

► Sell clothes you don't wear.

► Be a savvy sales shopper: not a tempted victim.

► Share with Mum: after all the Duchess of Cambridge did – remember the blue dress?

Travel

...between home and college

It's expensive. Make sure you never pay the full fare. We'll tell you how to cut your costs by planning your journey and much more besides in Chapter 6, which looks at money-saving strategies.

i advice note

If you are a Scottish student living away from home, you can claim for three return journeys per year to your place of study, plus additional term-time travel to and from your institution. (This does not include students whose parents live outside the UK.) The first £159 of any claim will be disregarded. Only the most economical fares will be allowed and the cost of a student railcard or bus pass may also be reimbursed. Travel expenses are means-tested on family income.

Term-time travel

Walk. There is no better way to save. It's free and good for you. Many students say that walking is their main way of getting about. If you have accommodation close to your college you may not have to use public transport much at all. If your university is not city centre, or your accommodation is a long way out, this may not be an option and costs can rise. Get a bike. Failing that, look for special student bus passes.

London students often have the highest term-time travel bills. Most students are eligible for a discounted travelcard on the bus and tube which gives them a 30% discount.

What universities estimate travel costs students:

- ▶ Bristol £150 per annum
- ▶ City University London £10–£30 per week (£400–£1,200 per annum)
- ▶ Imperial London £35 per week (£1,365 per annum)
- ▶ Kent £0–£390 per annum
- ▶ Manchester £500 per annum
- ▶ Oxford £220 per annum.

Thrift Tips

Save money on travel

- ▶ Look for special deals.
- ▶ Book up early trips to and from university – there may be special deals available.
- ▶ Compare coach and train prices.
- ▶ Check if there is a different route you can take.
- ▶ Invest in stout walking boots.
- ▶ Get a bike.
- ▶ Investigate local travelcards.
- ▶ Invest in a Young Person's (16–25) rail and/or 16–26 coach card and get a third off.
- ▶ Share taxis after a night out.

💣 cash crisis

Some banks offer student railcards as a freebie in their student package – a significant long-term saving if you use the train regularly.

For help if travelling abroad as part of your course see Chapters 3 and 8.

Own transport

About a fifth of students are thought to own a car or motorcycle. This estimate includes many mature students, who tend to drive longer distances than younger students during term. Petrol is an obvious cost. Check with your university whether they allow students to have cars on campus. Parking charges at some universities can be exorbitant.

Table 2.7. What university costs: Aled's student budget

Outgoings per term	
Accommodation/food	£00 (lives at home)
Snacks/lunch	£120
Socialising	£360
Football/gym	£90
Mobile	£60
Travel petrol	£420
Car expenses	£480 approx.
Parking at university	£49.20
Total	£1,579.20
Fees	£1,400
Anticipated debt	£12,000

Aled, third year, Sport Management, University of Glamorgan. Living at home. See how Aled is paying for the cost of university in Chapter 8.

Aled's Thrift Tips

Live at home.

Get books free of charge on Google online.

Can I afford to run a car?

If your only income is the standard funding for students, most rational people would say no. But since so many students do seem to have cars they must be managing it somehow. If you are living at home and have a long journey into college then a car may be a saving – certainly cheaper than living in rented accommodation.

Some other points to take on board before you make the decision.

▶ Travel from your home to your university will probably be cheaper by car, but you may find yourself going home many more times during term.

▶ You may also be acting as chauffeur to the party (charge for lifts), taking trips out at weekends and doing the supermarket run.

▶ Maintenance and upkeep: don't underestimate the bills: they can be astronomical, especially for an old car.

▶ Unavoidable costs include road tax, currently £130 yearly (£71.50 half-yearly) for cars under 1549cc and £215 per annum (£118.25 half-yearly) if registered before March 2001. For cars manufactured after March 2001 you'll be charged according to its CO2 emissions. There are 13 different bands, and costs range from zero up to £460 a year for a mighty gas-guzzler. See the internet for details. The annual MOT will cost you around £55; look for cut price deals on the internet. Halfords were offering half-price MOTs and Kwik-Fit were even cheaper with a service.

▶ AA or RAC membership (expensive but a sensible precaution if your car has a tendency to break down).

▶ Insurance: students lucky enough to have a car may find they don't have much luck getting insurance, especially if they are first-time drivers and aged under 21. Shop around. Insurance costs vary, depending not just on who you are, but on where you live. Big city drivers pay a higher premium. Insurance premiums are based on the address where the car resides for the majority of the year. For you that's probably your university town.

- ▶ Petrol: look for cheap deals.
- ▶ Parking fees at university: parking is like gold dust. Every university has different rules. Most don't give parking to students in halls of residence unless they are disabled. Those living further from university might be lucky (seven mile radius or more). Even then there is a cost: from £1 a day at Birmingham and £1.10 at Glamorgan to £30 for 12 days (per calendar month) at Warwick. Leicester simply says no student parking. If having a car at university is important to you, check the parking regulations when you apply.

---

i advice note

A word of caution: think twice about 'fronting' – that's the old trick of mum taking out the insurance and naming the student as second driver. If there's a claim and it's discovered that the student is really the main driver, you could find the insurance company won't pay up.

Where is the cheapest place to study?

With no fees to pay, Scottish students who live and study in Scotland win hands down. Those from Wales and Northern Ireland can also make a good saving on fees. If you take fees out of the cost equation, then accommodation is the next major factor in determining your costs. And as you can see from Table 2.1 on page 28 a little luxury can cost you dear, in fact nearly £1,600 a year extra.

Actual living costs depend a great deal on the individual and how good they are at managing their money and how determined they are to save. Of course there are places where it is cheaper to live. Out of town is generally more cost effective than the city centre. Wales is definitely cheaper than the South East of England.

Taking the table below as a very rough guide, Glamorgan in Wales seems the cheapest place to be while London predictably is higher than them all when it comes to living costs.

Table 2.8. How much do the costs depend on where you live?

University costs per month	Newcastle	Glamorgan	Imperial London	Sussex	Glasgow Caledonian
Rent	£250–£360	Halls £340 Private £200	£500	£254–£570	£350–£450
Food + household	£175	£136	£200 incl. utilities	£220	£200
Socialising/personal	£200	£160	£200	£110	£100
Utilities	£60	£40	See above		£55
Mobile/Phone	£30	£28		£20–£40	£45
Course costs	£45	£40	£40	£60	£40
Insurance	£20	£4		£5	
Travel	£35	£20	£140	£5 local	£55
Total	£815–£925	£628–£768	£1,080	£674–£1,010	£845–£945

The student budgets scattered throughout this chapter will have given you some idea of what university is costing students today (before the great fee hike). In the next chapter we look at some of the courses which offer not only fee savings but help with maintenance costs as well.

3 Making the right course choice

This chapter looks at how your course choice and the way you study can affect your finances and your future. It helps you to consider:

- ▶ courses which offer special fee or funding savings
- ▶ courses which have higher cost implications
- ▶ studying abroad: is it a viable cost-saving option?
- ▶ course choices that could help secure your future employment and career prospects.

Your country needs you!

Some qualifications attract more funding than others. This is generally because they lead to careers where there is either a shortage of qualified people or they are important to the country. Healthcare courses fall into this category and there is no doubt what's on offer from the NHS will really cut your debt to a minimum.

Healthcare courses

Students on these NHS-funded degree courses have no fees to pay:

- ▶ nursing
- ▶ midwifery
- ▶ operating department practice.

Allied healthcare students studying the following also have no fees:

- dietetics
- occupational therapy
- operating department practice
- orthoptics
- orthoptics and prosthetics
- physiotherapy
- podiatry/chiropody
- radiography (diagnostic and therapeutic)
- speech and language therapy.

Training for NHS staff is now university based. Many universities offer approved pre-registration courses for NHS staff. Fees on these courses are paid for by the NHS for UK and EU students.

NHS grants, bursaries, loans

In addition, from 2012, nurses, midwives, operating department practitioners and allied healthcare professional students on approved courses will be eligible for the following:

- all students will receive a £1,000 non-repayable grant each year
- **plus** a means-tested bursary of up to £4,395 (£5,460 London), non-repayable
- non-means-tested repayable loans are also available up to £3,263 per annum (see Table 3.1).

! It's a fact

Now that nurses and midwifery staff in NHS hospitals will need to have a degree, Diploma courses will be phased out by September 2013.

Table 3.1. Nursing, midwifery and allied health professionals bursary and loan rates (England) (p.a.)

	Non means-tested grant	Means-tested bursary maximum rates	Loan rates for 2012	Total maximum
London	£1,000	£5,460	£3,263	£9,723
Living away from home	£1,000	£4,395	£2,324	£7,719
Living in parents' home	£1,000	£3,350	£1,744	£6,094

Scotland, Wales and Northern Ireland have comparable financial arrangements, although figures may vary slightly.

Extra allowances may be available for extra weeks of study, and also for older students, single parents, those who have dependants or students who incur clinical placement costs.

How the NHS finding system works

If you don't come from a low-income family (which means a household income of £25,000 or under) then your bursary is going to be means-tested. This means you probably won't receive the full amount listed above. A family income of over £42,600 and you won't receive any bursary at all. So what or who fills the gaping hole in your finances? The answer: parents, your partner, your own hard work, your university or a loan. Welcome to the squeezed middle!

To find out more:

▸ see Chapter 4 for information on university bursaries

▸ see Chapter 7 on how to earn extra cash

▸ see Chapter 8 for details of family contributions and loans.

For more information on NHS bursaries

England
Contact the NHS Student Grants Unit, 22 Plymouth Road, Blackpool
FY3 7JS, helpline: 0845 358 6655 or websites: www.nhscareers.nhs.uk or
www.nhsstudentgrants.co.uk.

Wales
Contact the NHS Student Awards Unit, 2nd floor, Golate House,
101 St Mary's Street, Cardiff CF10 1DX, telephone bursary enquiries:
029 2019 6167 or website: www.nliah.wales.nhs.uk.

Scotland
Contact the SAAS, Gyleview House, 3 Redheughs Rigg, South Gyle,
Edinburgh EH12 9HH, tel: 0131 476 8227 or 0845 111 1711, email:
saas.geu@scotland.gsi.gov.uk or website: www.saas.gov.uk.

Northern Ireland
Contact the Bursaries Administration Unit, Central Services Agency,
2 Franklin Street, Belfast BT2 8DQ or tel: 028 9055 3661, or contact the
appropriate ELB, websites: www.delni.gov.uk or www.dhsspsni.gov.uk.

Medical and dental students

Medical and dental students who are on a standard five- or six-year
course will be treated as any other student in that area of the UK for
the first four years of their course, so could be liable for fees of up to
£9,000 and would be eligible for student funding outlined later in
this book (see Chapters 4 and 8).

Fees in the first four years will depend on where you live, and where
you study. (See fee information in Chapter 1 for England, Wales,
Scotland and Northern Ireland.)

From Year 5 wherever you live or study in the UK, your fees will be
paid for by the NHS and you will be eligible for the NHS funding
package shown in the table on page 55 for other NHS staff.

By the fifth year, especially if you live and study in England, you may
well have ratcheted up some £60,000–£70,000 of debt. And even

with the NHS help you will probably need a loan which will increase your financial burden.

Graduate entry

Graduates embarking on the four-year fast track medical programme will have their fees paid by the NHS from the second year onwards and will also be eligible for the NHS funding package from that time (see page 55).

Fee reminder

Throughout the UK fees are £9,000 maximum, unless you:

► live and study in Northern Ireland (maximum £3,465)
► live and study in Scotland (£0 fees)
► live in Wales and study anywhere (maximum £3,465).

Courses which offer industrial placements

A year out in the real world on a paid industrial placement or internship is one of the best ways to help minimise your debt. The salary paid will depend on how many years' study you have completed and the company you join but you may get between £12,000 and £15,000.

A good industrial placement should offer so much more than just cash:

► valuable technical experience
► training
► opportunity to acquire new and useful skills
► opportunity to develop a relationship with industry
► chance to learn a new language if your placement is abroad
► a job offer when you graduate
► possible sponsorship for your final year.

Some courses include an industrial placement which could last between nine and 12 months. You will be informed of this when you apply to university. With other courses it is an optional extra.

Most universities will have a special work experience team who are on hand to give you full information on what is on offer. See page 19 for details about the fee structure for industrial placements.

Which courses offer an industrial placement?

Good engineers are always in demand. We just don't have enough of them. Most engineering degrees are for four years and often include an industrial placement year.

However, it's not just engineering degrees which include an industrial placement year. There are many others including Chemistry at Sussex, Biotechnology (BSc Hons) at Newcastle, and Pharmacology at Kingston to name but a few. At Loughborough some 16 different departments offer industrial placements. These include the School of the Arts, School of Business and Economics, Design and Technology, English and Drama, School of Sport, Exercise and Health Sciences as well as the more traditional Engineering, Physics and Information Technology.

If you are interested in taking an industrial placement year it's important to find out just how good your year in industry is likely to be. Could it lead to the type of employment you are looking for? And how strong are your university's links with industry – in other words can they deliver?

When choosing your course it is important to quiz university department heads closely before applying. Don't be overawed. In engineering it's a buyers' market. Find out:

- ► what links the university has with industry
- ► whether you will be certain of getting an industrial placement (not always guaranteed in these times of cutbacks)
- ► will the placement on offer develop your technical skill
- ► will you get paid? (in these times of austerity some companies just offer expenses, some nothing at all)

► what the course is really like by speaking to students already on the course – they will give you an honest appraisal.

Remember any industrial experience is part of your degree, and it can be as important as the academic work you do. For more on industrial placements see Chapter 7.

---

i **advice note**

Want to know the top university for the subject you want to study? See the university league tables on the Complete University Guide website: www.thecompleteuniversityguide.co.uk/league-tables.

Specialist courses

This section covers information on:

► social work
► dance and drama courses.

Degree in social work

The Social Work Bursary (see Table 3.2 on the next page) is available to students ordinarily resident in England studying on an approved undergraduate course (full or part time). You can find out whether your chosen course is one approved for funding by checking with the university or college before you make your application. You will still pay fees but the bursary is not income-assessed, which means that earnings, savings and other sources of income are not taken into consideration. It includes a basic grant (£575 of this is towards placement travel) and a fixed contribution towards practice learning opportunity (PLO)-related expenses and tuition fees.

Full details on eligibility criteria and funding availability can be found on the NHS website: www.nhsbsa.nhs.uk/swb.

Table 3.2. Rates of social work bursary available

	London-based HE institution	HE institution elsewhere
Full-time students subject to fees	£4,975	£4,575
Part-time students (depending on years of study)	Up to £2,985	Up to £2,745

Help from Student Finance may be available. Figures are for 2011–12, based on a 52-week period.

Social work bursary contacts

England
Website: www.nhsbsa.nhs.uk/swb or you can email swb@ppa.nhs.uk.
Alternatively, call the bursaries customer service team on 0845 610
1122.

Scotland
Bursaries are not available. Tel: 0845 60 30 891, website: www.sssc.
uk.com.

Wales
Scheme varies depending on where you are studying, tel: 0845 070
0249, www.ccwales.org.uk.

Northern Ireland
Tel: 028 9052 0517, website: www.dhsspsni.gov.uk.

Dance and drama

If you've got talent your motivation must be which is the best way
to exploit my gifts? *Cut the Cost of Uni's* aim is far more mundane –
which is the best funded route to take?

Route 1
At university this is the more traditional route. Funding is in place,
and though debt will always be on the horizon, your studies will be

secure. Students offered a place at a university to study for a degree in acting, music, or theatre studies will pay the fees demanded by the university and will be eligible for the standard funding for first degree students outlined in Chapters 4 and 8. And the more entrepreneurial might get some ideas of how to put their talents to good use from Chapter 7 which covers earning while you are learning.

Route 2

The Conservatoire for Dance and Drama is a higher education institution which brings together eight of our highest quality performing arts schools in the UK offering training in all aspects of dance and drama. These are:

- ▶ Bristol Old Vic Theatre School
- ▶ Central School of Ballet
- ▶ Circus Space
- ▶ London Academy of Music and Dramatic Art
- ▶ London Contemporary Dance School
- ▶ Northern School of Contemporary Dance
- ▶ Rambert School of Ballet and Contemporary Dance
- ▶ Royal Academy of Dramatic Art (RADA).

The Conservatoire has set fees at £9,000 per annum for a full-time, three-year, first degree course for UK and EU students; and £16,000 per annum minimum for overseas students.

The affiliated schools qualify for state funding. If you are offered a place you would be eligible for the same funding as other undergraduates in the UK from Student Finance England (or equivalent). See Chapters 4 and 8.

In addition to any state funding Conservatoire schools offer a range of scholarships. Most scholarships are given as a fee discount to reduce your overall debt on graduating, and some scholarships will be income assessed. Talent-awarded scholarships will be open to all eligible students.

To be considered for a scholarship you must indicate this on your application form to the school/s, and you must also complete an application form for Student Finance. The maximum fee discount will be £4,000 per annum.

For students in Scotland, Wales and Northern Ireland – authorities in these countries have their own financial support arrangements. Students from these areas will not be eligible for the Conservatoire's National Scholarship Programme.

Route 3

There are a number of private performing arts schools, some of whose qualifications are validated by a university. Of these schools, 21 institutions run courses that are validated by Trinity College, London and are eligible for the UK Government's Dance and Drama Awards funding scheme. The DirectGov website has a full list of these schools at www.direct.gov.uk/en/EducationAndLearning/14To19/MoneyToLearn/DanceandDrama/DG_066990.

Private performing arts schools which do not come under the state funding system do offer some form of funding to help with fees and living expenses. Competition for all these awards is very fierce and not all students who achieve a place will receive an award. Schools are also open to younger students.

If you are awarded a Dance and Drama Award, it will cover the majority of your tuition fees. However, you will also need to make a personal contribution. For the academic year 2011–12, this personal contribution was £1,275. The Dance and Drama Award is given regardless of your household income. Whether you receive any additional help depends on your circumstances.

If you are offered a place at a private college but are **not** given a Dance and Drama Award you will have to pay the full cost of the private tuition fee. For those who do not receive an award, fees could be £7,000–£13,000 per annum so a three-year course (including living costs) could set you back well over £50,000.

Students from England, Wales and Scotland may also be able to get help with living costs. How much extra will depend on your household income. Students from Northern Ireland should contact the student financial section at the Western ELB for help with fees and maintenance – email student.awards@welbni.org. Students from

EU countries should apply to their home country for help with living costs.

Dance and drama contacts

Conservatoire for Dance and Drama: www.cdd.ac.uk
Trinity College: www.trinitycollege.co.uk
Student Finance: www.direct.gov.uk/danceanddrama
Council for Dance Education and Training: www.cdet.org.uk

Courses which incur additional costs

Every course will incur some additional costs, such as:

- binding and specialist printing
- books
- computer and software
- computer disks and CDs
- computer paper
- memory sticks
- photocopying.

But there are courses which incur even higher additional costs and if you want to study that subject, many of these costs cannot be avoided. These include courses such as:

- architecture
- art, design and media
- other school of art and creative subjects
- biological sciences
- civil engineering
- commercial management and quantity surveying
- earth and environmental sciences
- geography

- geology
- international business studies
- sports science and exercise science/physics/management.

The list goes on. How much are we talking about? The examples below are extracts taken from the Loughborough and Portsmouth university websites (www.lboro.ac.uk; www.port.ac.uk). Both sites are worth visiting whether you are thinking of attending the university or not.

An important question to ask before applying to a university is: **what are the hidden extras?** To give you an idea, this is what Loughborough University is telling its students.

Table 3.3. Costs for one year (could be more in other years)

Course	Item(s)	Cost
BA Illustration	Initial purchase of materials	£115
	One-off payment to cover national study visit, international study visit, D&AD student membership, digital media specialists	£625
BA Fine Art	Starter tool kit	£60
	Workshop materials	£90
	Degree catalogue/publicity	£60
	Study visits	£115
	Optional overseas visits	£280–£490

Loughborough University

Table 3.4. Additional costs of trips during the course

Course	Cost
Marine Biology	£450
Civil Engineering and Surveying trips (3 diving trips)	£900
Geology and Earth Sciences	£800
Palaeobiology and Evolution	£750
Geological Hazards, Engineering Geology and Geotechnics	£1,100

University of Portsmouth

What help is available? Not a lot! See below for possible sources of funding.

- ▶ Try your university: scholarships to pay for travel/field trips may be available.
- ▶ Try your university's hardship fund.
- ▶ Reading University have a Donor Study and Travel fund to help students in real trouble with travel and field trips (not yet confirmed it will still be available in 2012–13). Other universities may have something similar.
- ▶ Try EGS (Educational Grants Service) and tap into the UK's wide range of trusts, and charitable award giving organisations, website: www.family-action.org.uk (see also Chapter 4).

Will my degree secure me a job?

The days are long gone when any degree would secure a job with a good company. In these days of austerity, with the prospect of unemployment staring you in the face, students need to be much more strategic in their degree choice and ask, not just what subject will get me where I want to go, but . . .

What subject would help ensure I find employment?

Higher Education Statistics Agency (HESA) statistics show that graduates in dentistry, medicine, nursing and veterinary medicine are the most likely to go straight into employment with annual earnings of between £22,000 and £31,000. If you are a graduate in one of the sciences, engineering, education or social work, your employment prospects also look good with over 50% of these graduates going straight into employment.

> **! it's a fact**
>
> Average graduate starting salaries for 2011–12 are predicted to go up by 4% to £26,000.
>
> Source: *AGR Graduate Recruitment Survey 2012 – Winter Review.*

But is having a degree in a needed subject enough to secure you a job?

Where should I study?

Bearing in mind the strong competition for diminishing job opportunities this is an important question to ask. *Cut the Cost of Uni* looked on the Complete University Guide website and found this list.

Table 3.5. Universities offering the best overall employment prospects

University	Recent graduates in employment
Imperial College London	86.7%
Cambridge	85.5%
Oxford	85%
London School of Economics	84.1%
Durham	80%
St Andrews	76.3%

Complete University Guide website

But when you ask the question where does the course/subject I want to study rank?, the picture can be radically changed.

Table 3.6. Universities offering best graduate prospects by subject area

Subject	Top UK universities according to www. thecompleteuniversityguide.co.uk
Accounting and finance	Bath, Warwick, London School of Economics
Art and design	Edinburgh, University College London, Oxford, Reading
Social work	Bath, Lancaster, York
Leisure	Surrey, Stirling, Strathclyde
Sports science	Loughborough, Durham, Edinburgh

Complete University Guide website

These are just examples. To find the answer for the subject you want to study do the following.

▶ Visit the Complete University Guide website: www. thecompleteuniversityguide.co.uk.

▶ Click onto league tables.

▶ Click onto the degree subject you are interested in.

▶ Discover, based on past data, which university offers the best graduate prospects for which subjects.

This is just one route to take. There are many different league tables around and all use different criteria to rank universities, subjects, job opportunities and salaries (see the Association of Graduate Recruiters' findings below). Look around, check out the internet and do your research before making a decision.

Table 3.7. Top graduate earners

Employment sector	Median graduate starting salary 2010–11
Investment banking and fund management	£39,000
Law	£37,000
Banking and financial services	£28,000
IT/Telecommunications	£26,000
Insurance	£26,000
Fast-moving consumer goods	£25,750
Energy, water or utility	£25,000
Accountancy or professional services	£24,750
Transport and logistics	£24,500
Engineering or industrial	£24,000
Retail	£24,000

AGR Graduate Recruitment Survey 2012 – Winter Review

No guarantee

Even studying the right subject at the right university isn't a guarantee of a job at the end. What employers are looking for are people with the extra skills, experience and the 'pizzazz' which marks them out as special. Something on your CV which lifts it out of the pile of mostly internet applications and says, 'this person is worth considering'. If you haven't got that extra something you aren't going to get past the first hurdle.

i advice note

Think industrial placements and internships (see page 19 and Chapter 7).
Think sponsorship (see Chapter 5).
Think work experience and additional skills (see Chapter 7).

Studying abroad as part of your course

As we said in Chapter 1, with the introduction of £9,000 fees in England, studying abroad is becoming an option that many more students are considering.

Certain courses will require that you study abroad for a year as part of your course. This could be a work secondment so you may well be earning, or studying at a university. You would then be eligible for UK funding (see Chapters 4 and 8) and this may possibly include extra travel costs.

Most of these secondments are taken under the auspices of the EU's Erasmus programme.

EU Erasmus

This programme is designed to encourage greater co-operation between universities and other higher education institutions in Europe. Erasmus assists students wanting to study or possibly work for up to a year in another EU country as part of their degree. The scheme is open to participating universities.

You don't have to be studying languages to benefit from the Erasmus programme. You may go on a work placement or study at a university for a period of 3–12 months.

You don't have to pay fees at your host university and you will continue to receive UK funding (loans, grants, bursaries) if studying.

Your maintenance loan may be increased if studying abroad to £6,535 maximum. If working you may also be given a grant towards extra expenses. The average grant over the last three years was €378 a month (roughly £307.98).

Students choosing less visited European countries last year, e.g. Bulgaria, Croatia, Cyprus, the Czech Republic, received an additional one-off payment of €400 (2010–11).

If studying a full year under the Erasmus scheme you will receive a fee waiver for your UK fees.

Course length

If your course abroad is longer than your course in the UK you will be eligible for more funding. The rate given is worked out on a year of only 30 weeks and three days. If you need to stay longer, you can increase your loan (see Chapter 8 for details). Obviously this would entail more costs.

Travelling for study abroad

If you need to travel abroad to study (to Japan from Leeds for example) you can get help with travel costs but not for the full fare. Your loan already includes some travel element (approximately £300 in England, Wales and Northern Ireland); anything over this will be taken into consideration when calculating how much grant and loan you are entitled to receive. It is probably best to let Student Finance calculate your entitlement.

Remember when claiming for costs to give all the facts – the journey from your home to the airport costs something, too. (Arrangements differ in Scotland, where the disregarded amount is around £159.)

Who to contact

Try your university as funding from Erasmus is arranged mainly through your university or college. They should have full information and should therefore be your first point of call. Otherwise, contact the Erasmus organisation via the British Council.

For more information visit the website: www.britishcouncil.org/erasmus, for general enquiries tel: 0161 957 7755, for administrative enquiries tel: 029 2092 4311.

'Students who have a compulsory study period abroad can get into serious financial difficulties. Nobody warns you of the cost of this before you choose a course such as European Studies and Modern Languages.'
Third year, French and Russian

Will a year abroad save me money?

If it's an EU Erasmus year abroad it shouldn't cost you more than studying in the UK and it may well cost you less. You will certainly save on your fees. You should also receive a grant of around £307 a month to help with living costs, and you will still be eligible for the UK funding package. The cost of living in most EU countries is less than in the UK.

If you are going further afield for your Erasmus year abroad check out the many travel scholarships that are on offer through universities. For example:

► the BP International Elite Scholarship programme which offers 10 scholarships of £7,000 to student engineers spending an academic year in China or Malaysia. Or £1,500 for a summer school place

► Santander offers 15 £1,000 scholarships to students taking a study year in a Latin American country

► the Department for Business, Innovation and Skills offers Scholarships for Excellence which give undergraduate students from higher education institutions in England the opportunity to spend a semester or full year at a higher education institution in Hong Kong. A minimum of 10 scholarships will be awarded each year, with each scholarship worth up to £4,000.

Studying for your whole degree abroad

Fees have rocketed, so it is hardly surprising that more and more students are looking further afield to study for a degree. Last year some 22,000 British students were studying for degrees abroad (8,900 in the US) and this figure is set to rise. But is it really financially feasible to study for your whole degree in another country without financial backing from your family?

Studying in Europe

There is no doubt that apart from Scotland, fees in the UK are way above those in the rest of Europe, as you can see here.

Table 3.8. What tuition fees do European students pay?

Country	Tuition fees
Austria	No fees
Denmark	No fees
Finland	No fees
Greece	No fees
Hungary	No fees
Iceland	No fees
Ireland	No fees
Luxembourg	No fees
Norway	No fees
Slovenia	No fees
Sweden	No fees
Czech Republic	€1,000 (£832) per semester
France	€174 (£144) p.a. for a bachelor's degree €226 p.a. (£188) for a master's
Germany	€500 (£416) per semester but could vary depending on the state
Netherlands	€1,713 (£1,425) p.a.
Portugal	€1,250 (£1,040) p.a.
Spain	€570–€1,280 (£474–£1,065) p.a.
Switzerland	€750–€3,000 (£623–£2,496) per semester

In some countries a small registration fee is required. The question of fees is a constant topic of discussion in European countries. Always check for the current situation.

! It's a Fact

Students from Northern Ireland who cross the border into the Republic of Ireland to study will find that the €2,250 registration fee will be paid by the Northern Ireland Department of Employment and Learning.

Under EU law students from other EU countries have to be treated like home students regarding tuition fees. This means as a resident of the UK you will be treated like the students in the country where you are studying and will normally pay no tuition fees or very little.

You don't have to be a linguist

Many European universities offer a range of courses taught in English, so you don't have to be studying languages to study in Europe.

The best countries for providing degree courses taught in English are:

- ▶ Denmark
- ▶ Finland
- ▶ Republic of Ireland, of course
- ▶ Sweden
- ▶ The Netherlands.

These countries offer some courses taught in English:

- ▶ Czech Republic
- ▶ France
- ▶ Germany
- ▶ Hungary
- ▶ Iceland
- ▶ Italy
- ▶ Luxembourg
- ▶ Norway
- ▶ Portugal
- ▶ Switzerland.

So what is stopping all our young people from taking off across the channel to study?

The reality check: studying for a full degree in Europe

You need to consider the following points very carefully before making your decision.

- ▶ You are going to need money up front.
- ▶ Any fees charged will have to be paid before you start your studies.
- ▶ No fee doesn't necessarily mean no costs. Many universities have registration fees, and there are additional health and personal insurance costs, students' union fees and other expenses to consider.
- ▶ The most expensive part of your stay will be living costs; these depend on where you are studying. As in the UK, capital cities are more expensive places to live than country towns. European countries likely to be more expensive than the UK:
  - ▶ Belgium
  - ▶ Iceland
  - ▶ Netherlands
  - ▶ Norway
  - ▶ Sweden
  - ▶ Switzerland.
- ▶ Accommodation: halls of residence are generally cheaper but not all European universities have them. The cost could be similar or possibly higher than in the UK.
- ▶ You will need to eat. Top tip: learn to shop and eat like a local.
- ▶ Living costs in the UK are generally between £7,000 and £8,000 per annum (£583–£667 per month). You should anticipate at least this amount, and being far from home it could be more. Example costs of living in Europe:
  - ▶ Czech Republic: £172 per month
  - ▶ France (Paris): £862 per month, less elsewhere
  - ▶ Germany: £663 per month
- ▶ The university you attend may need to know how you are going to finance your stay before they will give you a place. That means having finance organised. Part-time work is generally not considered an answer.

► Don't forget health insurance. You will need to have a European Health Insurance Card (EHIC) which allows you to access state-provided healthcare in the European Economic Area. It's free from the NHS. But this alone may not be enough. You will need to check with your university.

► Unlike students taking a year abroad as part of their degree, you will not benefit from the UK's funding scheme so there would be no grants, bursaries and loans from the UK government to back you up while you studied for your degree. Any fees you did have to pay would need to be paid up front and the rest would be 'pay as you go'.

► So you will have to fund yourself. Or survive on funding from your chosen university – **if there is any!**

! It's a fact

As the University of London Institute in Paris is part of the University of London, the institute's three-year French course can be studied in Paris, but you would be treated as a UK student and be eligible for UK funding. The downside is you would liable for UK fees. (See funding details in Chapter 4.)

But don't be put off – see below for the benefits.

Savings and plus points of studying for your degree abroad

Scholarships for students from abroad are available but competition is high. See www.scholarshipportal.eu to search for scholarships that may be available to you. You should also check out your university of choice to see if they have any funding for international students.

While travel from your home to university could be expensive, you will probably not be popping home each weekend. European countries are often more student-friendly and you may find excellent travel discounts and concessions on buses and trains.

As an EU citizen you will have a legal right to work, if you can find it. However, don't rely on funding your degree on earnings which may never materialise. Visit the country and see what's available.

You may find less popular countries of study such as the Czech Republic, Bulgaria and Croatia are cheaper places in which to live.

Many countries have special arrangements for their students, such as concessionary rates for meals and accommodation and as an EU student studying in an EU country you would benefit from these.

> **Verdict:** if you can raise the cash, your university costs could be reduced by half compared with the UK.

The Netherlands: student funding scheme

Students who work for at least 8 hours a week in the Netherlands are entitled to a state grant of €266 a month. The University of Maastricht, Holland offers EU students a great deal providing you are prepared to work hard.

▶ Basic grants of €226 per month are awarded if you work at least 32 hours a month.

▶ The grant includes a free travelcard.

▶ The basic grant is a debt-free gift providing you graduate. Fail and it has to be paid back along with the cost of the travelcard.

▶ Fees are €1,771 per annum. Will increase substantially if you fail to graduate and decide to extend your course period.

▶ Minimum wage depends on age, increasing each year.

See www.ib.greop.nl for more information.

Table 3.9. University of Maastricht student funding scheme

Funding on offer (per month)	
Basic grant	€266.23 (£219.43)
Supplementary grant	€244.60 (£201)
Loan	€283.86 (£233)
Tuition fee loan	€147.58 (£121)
Total	€942.27 (£774.43)
Average pay: 32 hours work per month (based on minimum wage at 20)	€172.88 (£142.04)

Note: as we go to press the Netherlands are preparing for an election. There is talk of increasing the hours students can/must work, but also the whole funding systems could change. Be aware and keep up to date with any changes.

Table 3.10. Monthly cost of living in Maastricht, Holland

Rent	€300 (£247)
Food	€180 (£148)
Books/equipment	€40 (£33)
Insurance	€98 (£80)
Clothes/personal expenses	€95 (£78)
Leisure	€100 (£82)
Total per month	€813 (£668)
Plus fees per month	€147.58 (£121)
Total living costs and fees	€960.58 (£789)

This is just one example so do your research and see whether similar incentives are available at other European universities.

A word of caution: don't let the glamour of studying abroad cloud your judgement. While many EU universities have a high reputation for their academic standards, make sure the quality of the degree course you are taking meets those high standards and will help, not hinder, your future career.

Studying in the US

The US has always been popular with students. Some 8,900 British students were studying there in 2010–11 and many more cross the pond for work experience. Now in this current climate of higher fees at home, the US is looking an even more attractive proposition.

A year of study with maintenance costs at a good/Ivy League university in the US would realistically cost around £37,000 per annum ($60,000) and that's without travel, compared with an estimated cost of £17,500 in the UK.

You might think the costs still favour the UK, along with the ease of finding funding. Remember the UK funding package is not available if you study abroad so you will need to have funds up front and will probably need parental backing to see you through.

> ## ! It's a Fact
>
> Is the US too expensive for study? Not a bit of it, the US could be the cheapest option of all.

However, American universities are often well endowed and offer many scholarships and grants to students. You could be awarded up to £6,000, cutting your actual fees to around £10,000 per annum. Bear in mind the following:

▶ competition for international scholarships can be high

▶ scholarships are generally given for academic excellence, or for a special talent especially in sport.

You might think top US universities are out of your reach. But don't just look at the headline figures. Top Ivy League universities such as Yale, Harvard and Princeton have a completely different attitude to funding from the UK. They are primarily interested in attracting the best, most gifted students no matter where in the world they come from. And that could include you.

Their attitude: apply, and if you are sufficiently gifted to get in then we'll worry about the funding. Taking Yale as an example this is how their system works.

▶ They start by calculating all your costs: fees, maintenance, accommodation, food, personal needs, travel (which for British students means flights from the UK) and come up with a figure.

▶ They then deduct what they think your family can afford to contribute.

If family income is:

- ► $65,000 or less (approximately £41,000): contribution zero
- ► $65,000–$130,000 (£41,000–£81,164): contribution 1%–10% of income
- ► $130,000 (£81,164) and above: contribution 10%–20% of income.

Many things are taken into consideration when calculating family income and family contribution including siblings at college.

- ► They also look at your income. By this they generally mean your potential earnings while studying. Most students work on or around the campus, for around 8 hours a week, at a wage of $11.75 per hour – it's not peanuts. Likely estimate is $376 per month (£241 per month; £2,892 per annum). They come up with what they call your 'need' figure and this is what you would get.

So you might find you receive one of the best educations from one of the top universities in the world absolutely free.

Taste the difference! Free US summer school

Find the idea of the US degree option difficult to believe? The Sutton Trust have been running a programme of summer schools actually in the US to give the brightest students, along with non-privileged students from state schools, a taster of what a US university is like by taking them to Yale University for a week with all expenses paid. See www.suttontrust.com/us-summer-school.

Start your search early: ideally 18 months before you want to go

If funding help from your US university is essential, make sure you ask what is on offer when you apply. Applications have to be made to each individual university – there is no umbrella organisation like UCAS so it can be an expensive and time-consuming business.

A levels are not enough: admissions exams have to be sat – these can be done in this country but again there is a cost implication. Universities may offer special loan facilities to parents to help pay their contribution. Student loans in the US can be tricky. Always read the small print.

Once you are there

US universities are vast, often like small towns, you can get lost and lonely.

Student part-time employment is possible but the law in the US for international students is fuzzy.

- ▶ Year 1: allowed to work up to 20 hours per week but only on the university campus
- ▶ Year 2 onwards: can probably work off campus but this is not certain and not necessarily a right.

US degrees are generally 4–6 years. The first two years of a degree cover a wide range of topics and not just your specialism. This time can be spent in a cheaper 'community college', but make sure you know what you are getting into. Do your research before you go.

For further information contact the Fulbright Commission (www. fulbright.co.uk/study-in-the-USA). It holds annual fairs which universities from all over the USA attend so you can find out first hand exactly how much it would cost and where you could find funding. These are usually held in September in London.

Other English-speaking countries

Other English-speaking nations such as Australia, New Zealand and Canada are a possibility for study, but not in the context of cutting the cost of university.

Australia. We like the lifestyle, but the fees are comparable with the worst in the UK. Bachelor's: A$14,000–A$35,000 (£8,805–£22,012) per annum. The cost of living is high, and competition for scholarships is fierce. If you are determined to go, start your research early. Visit www.studyinaustralia.gov.au.

New Zealand. The fees are a little better: NZ$18,000–NZ$25,000 (£8,612–£11,961) per annum. Allow around £8,000 per annum for living costs. Scholarships are not easy to come by. See www. newzealandeducated.com.

Canada. They tend to see themselves as a cheaper option compared with other English-speaking countries, which could be true. Fees range from C$8,000 to C$26,000 (£4,938 to £16,049) per annum. Scholarships are available, but again difficult to come by and getting there isn't going to be cheap. Find out more at www.studyincanada.com.

Research, research, research

You can't know too much! Whether you opt for Europe, the US, Australia, Canada, New Zealand or somewhere less well travelled the answer to a successful stay is research. You need to know:

- ▶ what to expect
- ▶ what it will cost
- ▶ where the money will come from
- ▶ that it will be there when you need it
- ▶ how you are going to maintain yourself and live through the holidays
- ▶ whether you can work
- ▶ what to do in an emergency
- ▶ where to turn if the money runs out.

You need to have Skype, a mobile phone, email, a sympathetic parent at the ready for when you need to hear a friendly voice from home – it will happen. Above all, you should start your search early: we advise at least 12–18 months before you want to go.

Information about studying abroad

- ▶ UNESCO publication *Study Abroad* (available on www.amazon.co.uk)
- ▶ *Studying Abroad: A guide for UK students* by Cerys Evans, Trotman Publishing, 2012 (www.trotman.co.uk)
- ▶ UK Socrates–Erasmus, tel: 029 2092 4311 or website: www.britishcouncil. org/erasmus
- ▶ Save the Student, website: www.savethestudent.org/study-abroad
- ▶ Fulbright Commission, website: www.fulbright.co.uk
- ▶ The Student World, website: www.thestudentworld.com/study_abroad

There are fairs where you can meet representatives from over 60 universities from around the world. For details go to the Student World website and click on fairs.

4 Debt-free funding: where to find it and how to get it

Everybody likes a freebie and this is what this chapter is basically about – funding you don't have to pay back.

The first three chapters have really looked at what university is likely to cost, now we can start to look at how you are going to pay for it, ideally by discovering all the opportunities for debt-free funding that are available and what you need to do to get them.

As the awards we are talking about here are the kind you don't need to pay back, it makes sense to pursue these options before even considering taking out a loan. This chapter will look at:

- ▶ maintenance grants
- ▶ bursaries
- ▶ scholarships
- ▶ other awards.

What are your options?

The two main elements of debt-free student maintenance are maintenance grants and university bursaries.

Not every student gets everything. How much support and in particular debt-free support you can receive will depend on three factors:

1. where you live
2. family income
3. where you choose to study.

Non-repayable maintenance grants

The facts

- All four countries in the UK give maintenance grants of varying amounts.

- Maintenance grants are non-refundable and are quite different from maintenance loans, which you do have to pay back.

- Maintenance grants are given to students from low-income families. Figures vary slightly depending on where you live.

- Generally the more grant you get the less maintenance loan you are entitled to (see Chapter 8 for loans).

Maintenance grants in England

Whether you get anything will depend on your family's income. If it's £25,000 or below you will receive the full amount on offer: £3,250 per annum. If it's over £42,600 you will receive nothing. If your family income falls between those figures, the award given is on a sliding scale. Table 4.1 below gives approximate figures.

Table 4.1. Maintenance grants for new students in England: who will receive what in 2012–13

Family income	Grant
£25,000 or less	£3,250
£30,000	£2,341
£35,450	£1,432
£40,000	£523
£42,600	£0

It is thought that around a third of students in England will receive a full grant and around a third a partial grant.

Student Finance England will calculate how much a student will receive, based on the information you supply on your application form for funding. Maintenance grants are paid in three instalments, one at the start of each term.

Maintenance grants in Wales

All Welsh domiciled students from lower-income families, wherever they study in the UK, will be able to apply for a Higher Education Assembly Grant of up to £5,000 per annum to help with maintenance.

This is a much higher figure than anywhere else in the UK and it does not have to be paid back. It is however means-tested and operates in a similar way to the grant in England.

Amounts available in Wales:

► income of £0–£18,370, a full grant of £5,000 will be given
► income of £18,371–£50,020, a partial grant between £5,000 and £50 will be given depending on family income
► family income over £50,020, no grant will be given.

For further information see www.studentfinancewales.co.uk.

Table 4.2. Maintenance grants for Welsh domiciled students

Family income	Grant p.a.
£18,370 or less	£5,000
£25,000	£3,242
£30,000	£2,033
£34,000	£1,106
£40,000	£711
£50,020	£50

Maintenance grants in Northern Ireland

The basic grant in Northern Ireland is £3,475, which is slightly higher than in England but lower than in Wales. The grant is means-tested. A full grant is given where the family income is

£19,203 or less. The grant is then given on a sliding scale up to a maximum income of £41,065 – whether you study in Northern Ireland or anywhere in the rest of the UK.

A means-tested grant for maintenance of up to £2,000 is available for students studying in the Republic of Ireland.

Table 4.3. Maintenance grants for Northern Ireland domiciled students

Family income	Grant
£19,203 or less	£3,475
£25,000	£2,201
£30,000	£1,215
£35,000	£689
£41,065	£0

Maintenance grants in Scotland

Rather than a grant, it is called the young student's bursary in Scotland, and the amount given is less than in the rest of the UK. The maximum bursary of £2,640 is given where household income is £19,310 or less. The amount will then reduce depending on income to zero where household income is over £34,195.

These figures are for students studying in Scotland. If you are a Scottish student and studying outside Scotland, then the figures are rather different.

Table 4.4. Maintenance grants for Scottish students

Family income	Studying in Scotland	Bursary if studying outside Scotland
£19,310 or less	£2,640	£2,150
£20,000	£2,518	£2,050
£23,000	£1,986	£1,617
£29,000	£921	£750
£32,000	£389	£317
£34,195	£50	£50
£35,000	£0	£0

See Table 4.5 below to find out which UK region gets the best deal on maintenance.

Table 4.5. Cut the cost of uni: with a grant for low-income families

Region	Maximum grant given	Income above which full grant starts to decrease	Income above which no grant given
England	£3,250	£25,001	£42,600
Wales	£5,000	£18,371	£50,020
Northern Ireland	£3,475	£19,204	£41,065
Scot studying in Scotland	£2,640	£19,310	£34,195
Scot studying outside Scotland	£2,150	£19,310	£34,195

Applying for a maintenance grant

You should start thinking about applying for financial support as soon as you have applied for a place on a course. Do not wait until you have a confirmed place, just quote the course you are most likely to attend.

Make sure you apply even if you don't think you will be entitled to a maintenance grant as you will also be assessed for how much loan you are entitled to and how much (if anything) your family is expected to contribute.

What you receive will be calculated on the information you give. So make sure you fill in the form accurately. It is also important that parents provide accurate information.

Any university bursary you are entitled to will probably be based on your student finance assessment. Therefore as well as filling in the form accurately make sure you have also filled in the section which gives permission for financial information to be passed to your university so they can assess you for a university bursary (for more details see page 88).

How to apply in England

1. The Student Finance service should be online from December prior to the year you want to start your course. You can apply at www.direct.gov.uk/studentfinance, or you can download an application form to print out from the website or phone 0845 300 5090 to get one sent to you.

2. Fill in your application form and return it on the web or by post to Student Finance England. The address is on the website and the form. Give all the details you are asked for and say whether you intend to apply for a loan. Remember you may be asked to include:

   ▶ your National Insurance number

   ▶ details of your university course

   ▶ bank details

   ▶ passport

   ▶ parents' or partner's details including their NI number and income.

3. Once Student Finance England has received your application, you will be assessed to see what finance you are entitled to. You will then be notified by letter of what your entitlements are – this should be within six weeks of your application being received. You will be given a customer reference number and password so you can track the progress of your application and manage your own student finance account online. If you get in a muddle or need some advice, just log on to their helpful webchat service or secure messaging.

4. Before you start your course, you will be sent a payment schedule showing when you can expect to receive money. Timing is important.

Important points to note

New students applying for finance that depends on household income should get their application in by 31 May. Late applications may result in late payments.

If your circumstances change after this date you should let Student Finance know as soon as possible. You can do this by filling in a 'change of circumstances' form, which can be downloaded from the Student Finance website.

If you want to discover what help you are entitled to, check out the online calculator at www.direct.gov.uk/studentfinance.

How to apply in Scotland

Go to www.saas.gov.uk/student_support. If you prefer the paper method, however, go to Guides and Forms on the website and download what you need. Alternatively, phone 0845 111 1711 or 0845 111 0243, email saas.geu@scotland.gsi.gov.uk, or write to (or even visit) SAAS, Gyleview House, 3 Redheughs Rigg, Edinburgh EH12 9HH.

The deadline for applications for financial support for students starting courses between 1 August 2012 and 31 March 2013 is 31 March 2013. If you want your funding to be in place when you start your course you needed to apply by 30 June 2012. These dates are likely to reflect future application deadlines.

How to apply in Wales

You can apply for support online by logging on to www.studentfinancewales.co.uk, or you can make a paper application by contacting your local authority for a form or downloading a form from 'Forms and Guides' on the Student Finance Wales website. As with the English application procedure, once you have registered you will be given a customer reference number and password so you can track your account online.

Applications for support that depends on family income should be submitted by the start of May (for 2012 it was 4 May).

How to apply in Northern Ireland

The student finance applications system goes live around Easter at www.studentfinanceni.co.uk. You can request an application form from your local Student Northern Ireland office. You do not have to wait until you have a confirmed place on a course to apply. Return the application form, making sure you provide all the information requested.

Applications for support that depends on family income should be submitted ideally by mid-May (in 2012 it was 11 May).

University bursaries

What are they?

The Office of Fair Access (England) defines a bursary as 'a cash award where a student's eligibility is either wholly or partially dependent on their assessed household income.' So if you receive a full grant you'll probably also be eligible for a debt-free bursary.

Universities have always offered bursaries, especially for students from low-income families, but in this section, we'll explore the income-related bursaries on offer, for each of the devolved countries.

For details of charitable awards see page 111 and of scholarships see page 106.

National Scholarship Programme in England

To ensure access to our universities for students from low-income families the government has stipulated that English institutions wanting to charge fees of £6,000 or over must sign up to an 'access agreement', and participate in the National Scholarship Programme (NSP).

The NSP ensures that English students, attending English institutions, who receive the full maintenance grant (i.e. those from lowest-income families, see Table 4.5 on page 85) are given a further non-repayable bursary of at least £3,000, which makes a grand total of £6,250 free funding (combined maintenance grant and bursary).

How the funding is distributed is up to each individual university. It could be:

▶ a fee waiver

▶ a free foundation year if appropriate

▶ a discount on accommodation

▶ cash.

It's likely to be a mixture of the above since, under the NSP, students from families where income is £25,000 or less should receive no less than £3,000, of which only £1,000 can be given in cash. At most institutions you do have a say in how you want to receive your funding.

i **advice note**

Most financial pundits say go for cash/maintenance. Unless you know for certain you are going to be a high-earning success story the fee waiver is unlikely to reduce the amount of debt you actually repay. So you won't feel the benefit. But you would if you took the cash now. The decision is a matter of balancing the probable against the possible. A difficult call!

Table 4.6. Cut the cost of uni: with maximum free funding in England

Outgoings	With no debt-free funding	With debt-free funding
Fees	£9,000	£9,000
Accommodation	£4,500	£4,500
Living expenses	£4,000	£4,000
Total income	£17,500	£17,500
Debt-free maintenance grant		−£3,250
Debt-free university bursary		−£3,000
Total		£11,250
Saving p.a.		£6,250

Some universities will stick to the guidelines giving bursaries just to students who receive the full maintenance grant. Others will offer them on a sliding scale to all those receiving a proportion of the maintenance grant. So shop around. There are some fantastic bursary deals about, and every university has a different approach. Finding a university giving generous bursaries could be more cost-effective than trying to find a low-cost course, and probably better educational value too.

Go to www.direct.gov.uk and search for 'bursaries, scholarships and awards' which has a list of universities and colleges taking part in the

NSP. NSP funding cannot be used by Welsh, Scottish or Northern Irish students. Details of bursaries for these students can be found on pages 91–95. Details of the NSP could change next year. However, the government is committed to doubling the amount it contributes next year.

Fee waiver saver: how it works

Manchester University's NSP scheme is typical:

Foundation year
- Award £5,000 max
- £4,000 fee discount plus £1,000 cash

Year 1
- Award £3,000 max
- £2,000 fee or accommodation discount plus £1,000 cash

Year 2 and subsequent years
- Award £2,500 max
- £2,500 as fee discount or as cash or split

Points to remember

Many universities ask the Student Loans Company to administer their bursary programme so you may be assessed for entitlement when you apply for government funding. This is not always the case. In the past many students found they were missing out on bursaries just because they didn't ask.

Check with your university if you don't receive what you think you are due. Bursaries are not necessarily given automatically and mistakes happen.

Important: as mentioned earlier make sure you have filled in the section on your application form which gives permission for financial information to be passed to your university so it can assess you for a university bursary.

For further information look at the university prospectuses and websites – these are a good starting point for finding out about university bursaries and scholarships and what you could be entitled to.

Crossing borders

As we have already said, universities in Wales, Scotland and Northern Ireland have decided to keep reduced fees or no fees for their home students while charging high fees, in many cases the maximum £9,000, to students from the rest of the UK.

As they still want to attract good students from the rest of the UK each university has implemented its own university bursary scheme which is only open to students coming in from outside the country. Here are a few examples.

Bursary schemes offered by universities in Scotland to students from outside the region

Since Scotland no longer gives students from the rest of the UK reduced fees, Scottish universities have implemented the RUK (Rest of UK) scholarship/bursary scheme to encourage students from the rest of the UK to study in Scotland. RUK is more an umbrella title than an actual scheme since every university offers something different; see examples below.

At **Edinburgh University** bursaries are offered on a sliding scale depending on family income. A bursary of £7,000 would be given where the family income is £16,000 or below, and this drops gradually to a bursary of £500 at an income of £42,600. Above this income figure no bursary is given.

The bursary can be used for either fees or maintenance. Students who receive the full low-income grant from their home country and live in university accommodation will receive a further non-repayable £1,000 towards the costs in their first year.

A further access bursary of at least £1,000 is available for those in financial need.

Table 4.7. Cut the cost of uni: with debt-free funding from Edinburgh University

Outgoings	With no free funding	With free funding
Fees	£9,000	£9,000
Accommodation	£4,500	£4,500
Living expenses	£4,000	£4,000
Total	£17,500	
	Debt-free maintenance grant (student from England)	−£3,250
	Debt-free university bursary	−£7,000
Additional bursary if living in university accommodation (first year only)		−£1,000
	Total	£6,250
	Saving p.a.	£11,250

The fees at **Glasgow University** are set at £6,750 and students have the choice of taking a four-year degree or an accelerated three-year course. Students studying on a standard 4–5 year course will be eligible for a £1,000 Glasgow Welcome bursary in their first year. This can be taken as a fee discount or cash bursary.

Students from low-income households will be eligible for either a fee discount or cash scholarship. A bursary of £2,000 would be given where family income is under £20,000; a bursary of £1,000 for an income of £20,001–£30,000; a bursary of £500 for an income of £30,001–£42,600. Above this level, no bursary is given.

Table 4.8. Cut the cost of uni: with full debt-free funding at Glasgow. Based on 2012 figures

Outgoings	three year degree + free funding	four year degree + free funding
Fees	£20,250	£27,000
Accommodation	£13,500	£18,000
Living expenses	£12,000	£16,000
Total	£47,750	£61,000
Income		
Debt-free maintenance grant (Eng)	−£9,750	− £13,000
Debt-free university grant	−£6,000	−£8,000
Welcome bursary (first year)	n/a	−£1,000
Total	£30,000	£39,000
Total saving on a three-year course	£9,000	

St Andrews University has a completely different take altogether. Here £7,500 is the magic figure which they think all students need to live on. This is arrived at by taking the non-repayable grant students receive plus the loan and then topping it up with a university bursary to a total of £7,500. So the calculation looks like this.

Table 4.9. Cut the cost of uni: with the university bursary scheme at St Andrews

Family income	Grant + loan	University bursary
£25,000	£7,125	£375
£30,000	£6,671	£829
£42,600	£5,525	£1,975

It may look a bit upside down compared with other schemes but it is fair.

Because St Andrews also wants to ensure access to the university for the brightest and the best from all regions some 50 bursaries of up to £2,000 per annum are offered to alleviate financial hardship to Scottish domiciled students with a household income of £42,600 or less.

Bursary schemes offered by Welsh universities to students coming in to study from the rest of the UK

As full fees of £9,000 per annum are generally charged by universities in Wales, each university has its own scheme to attract students from the rest of the UK.

Cardiff University for example offers bursary awards based on the amount of government funding a student receives. If household income is £30,000 or below the university will top up the grant and loan received to make £7,500.

If family income is between £30,001 and £42,000 the university will top up received funding to £6,750.

Aberystwyth has a fascinating calculator which increases your bursary/scholarships depending on your situation, course and special skills. For example:

▶ sitting an entrance exam: up to £1,200

▶ course excellence bursary: up to £666

▶ staying in halls: up to £800

▶ low household income: £1,100

▶ playing sport: £500

▶ playing an instrument: £500.

Tick all the right boxes (note this is only an example) and you could be looking at a bursary of £4,766 in your first year.

Bursary schemes offered by universities in Northern Ireland to students coming in from the rest of the UK

Queen's Belfast offers scholarships to students paying the full £9,000 fees who make Queen's their first choice. There are two levels and how much you receive is based on your ability:

▸ achiever grade (must achieve offer grades): £1,250 deducted from fees, so you pay £7,750

▸ top grade (AAB at A level): £2,500 deducted from fees, so you pay £6,500.

For more information on scholarships and bursaries check www.thecompleteuniversityguide.co.uk and www.direct.gov.uk/en/EducationAndLearning/UniversityAndHigherEducation/StudentFinance/Typesoffinance/DG_171571 and university websites.

Getting debt-free funding: Rachel's story

Rachel is 18 and a first-year BEd Primary Education student at Stranmillis University College, Belfast. When Rachel applied for funding from Student Finance she was hopeful that she would be entitled to a grant since she came from a one-parent family.

She received a £2,000 a year grant which is about two thirds of the maximum. She also asked for a student loan of around £3,000 per annum. This is paid in three tranches at the beginning of each term.

When her place at Stranmillis University College was confirmed they sent a form asking if she would 'like' a bursary. She was awarded £1,100 a year. No fee waiver or help with accommodation was suggested, but she was given cash which is paid in two tranches of £550 directly into her bank account.

As yet she does not feel the need to take out a fee loan, as her finances stretch. She lives in halls with full catering costing her £1,235 in her first term and £1,330 in her second. 'It is pretty basic,' she said. 'Ten student rooms to a corridor sharing a kitchen, two bathrooms, two showers and two toilets.'

She returns home at weekends: 'I don't feel I miss out on student life, most people go home. Campus is dead at weekends. It's like that in Northern Ireland.'

She borrows her mother's car to travel back and forth to university which costs her around £60 a fortnight on petrol. And her mother gives her another £300–£400 a term to help out with expenses. On top of this her dad chips in with £30 a month to help cover her £40 a month mobile phone bill.

Rachel has had a job since starting university. Initially she was earning £30 a week helping at a play centre on Saturdays but has now switched to piano teaching and increased her earnings to £40 a week.

Would she have gone to university without a grant and university bursary? 'Yes,' she says, 'but my final debt estimated at around £14,000 would have doubled.'

Rachel's income per annum

Grant: £2,000
Bursary: £1,100
Loan: £3,000
Mother: £1,050
Father: £360
Earnings: £1,440
Total: £8,950

💣 cash crisis

The NUS is calling for a national bursary scheme after a government survey showed a third of students based their higher education decisions on the amount of financial support available.

Receiving the money

Once you have registered your arrival at university and have started to attend the course, your university will notify the Student Loans Company and your student grant (and loan if applicable) will be paid into your bank account. So, it could take three working days after your institution has confirmed that you have arrived for the money to actually reach your bank account, so you may need funds to tide you over.

'I was living on £5 a week since an error had been made in processing my application form and I didn't receive my bursary until the last week of term.'

Second year, Biochemistry, Oxford

Arrangements for paying bursaries will depend on your university. They will probably notify you about the details when it is awarded.

If you have elected to receive your university bursary as cash, it is likely to be paid in two or three tranches at the beginning of term.

If your funding doesn't arrive

It can happen – fortunately not that often – but it can be dramatic when it does. In an ideal world, your cheque should be waiting for you when you arrive at your university or college, but things can go wrong. Some typical reasons we discovered were:

- wrong information on your bank account
- you didn't give all the information required, e.g. National Insurance number.

Whatever the reason, it doesn't help the destitute student to eat, so try the following options.

- Contact your bank. If you already have a bank account, they may help you out with a loan – most banks offer free overdrafts to students. Talk to the student adviser at the campus or local branch. This, of course, is no help to the first-year student who needs that cheque to open a bank account, so make sure you have an account before you start your course.
- Try your college. Ask them for temporary help. Most institutions have what's called a hardship fund set up to cover just this kind of eventuality.
- Try the Access to Learning Fund (or equivalent in Scotland, Wales, Northern Ireland). This has been set up to help students. Full details are given on page 103.
- Try your fellow students? They may well take pity on you when it comes to socialising, buying you the odd drink, but it is rarely a good idea to borrow from friends.
- Check your application online to see where it has got to and what is holding it up.
- Phone home and tap the bank of Mum and Dad.

Check the following 'special circumstances' to make sure you are not missing out

Siblings
What if I have a sibling claiming for funding?

If there are several children in higher education in the family then this is taken into consideration when calculating how much funding you and your siblings are entitled to. It may mean that even though the family income is over the threshold for a grant or a university bursary you may still get one.

Marriage
I'm thinking of getting married: will it affect my maintenance grant and loan entitlements?

Yes. Students who get married before the academic year are considered as independent and their support is no longer assessed on their parents' income but on that of their partner, provided he or she is earning enough.

I'm not married but living with a partner: will this affect my support?

Yes – you will be considered independent in the same way as a married student would be and income will be based on your partner's income.

Work
If I work part time, will it affect my student financial package?

No. Students can work during their course and the money earned will not be considered when their loan or grant is calculated.

Drop out
What will happen if I drop out of my course – will I have to pay back my grant and bursary?

You might; there are no set rules. As a rule of thumb the government and universities will waive completed terms but there could be a clawback for an uncompleted term.

Income support
If I become a full-time student will I still receive benefits such as income support?

If you get or qualify for income support or housing benefit you may be entitled to the special support grant instead of the maintenance grant (Welsh Assembly Grant in Wales). Whichever type of grant you receive the amount will be the same. The benefits from receiving a special support grant are:

▶ it won't reduce how much maintenance loan you can receive
▶ it doesn't count as income when calculating whether you are entitled to income-related benefits or tax credits.

This only applies to students from England, Wales or Northern Ireland, not those from Scotland.

Children
I have children to support: are there any other allowances, grants and bursaries I could apply for?

A non-repayable special support grant of up to £2,906 a year (£3,475 in Northern Ireland) is available for new full-time students who are eligible for benefits such as income support or housing benefit while they are studying. The main beneficiaries are likely to be lone parents, other student parents and students with disabilities. The grant is based on household income and does not have to be paid back if you're eligible for the maintenance grant. This will not affect any university bursary you are offered.

Additional support
The following grants are available to student parents.

▶ The parents' learning allowance: up to £1,508 per annum (£1,538 in Northern Ireland) helps with course-related costs for students with dependent children. This is income-assessed.

▶ The childcare grant: up to £148.75 a week for one child and £255 for two or more. The amount given is based on 85% of actual childcare costs. It is paid in three instalments by the Student Loans Company (SLC); it does not have to be repaid.

▶ Child tax credit: available to students with dependent children and paid by HMRC. Students receiving the maximum amount will be entitled to free school meals for their children. The amount you get will depend on circumstances. Call 0845 300 3900 for more details or visit www.hmrc.gov.uk/taxcredits and check out how much you could get.

▶ Adult dependants' grant: up to £2,642 per annum depending on your income and that of your dependants.

Leaving care
A one-off bursary of £2,000 could be available if you are leaving care. Get in touch with your local authority. Some universities

have special grants for students who have been in care. Ask when you apply.

Students with disabilities

If you are a higher education student with disabilities there are a number of ways you can get extra help, depending on your disability. If you follow up every lead offered here it's going to take time, but the results could be worthwhile.

The first thing you should do is choose your course, then choose the university or college where you would like to study. Next, check out the college facilities and their ability to cope with your specific disability by:

- ▶ requesting details of facilities
- ▶ visiting suitable institutions
- ▶ having a 'special needs' interview with the institution.

Then fill in your UCAS application. It's a good idea to start getting organised in the summer term of your first A level year as you may have to revise your choice of institution several times.

Disabled students' allowances

Disabled students' allowances (DSAs) are available for full- and part-time students and these offer support to those with a disability or specific learning difficulty such as dyslexia.

There are four types of DSA.

1. Up to £20,520 per year for non-medical personal help, e.g. readers, lip-speakers or note-takers (up to £15,390 if studying part time).
2. Up to £5,161 for the whole course for specialist course equipment, e.g. computer, word processor, Braille printer, radio microphone or induction loop system (whether studying full or part time).

3. A general DSA: up to £1,724 per year (up to £1,293 for part-time study) for minor items such as tapes, Braille paper or extra use of a phone.

4. Extra travel costs incurred as a result of your disability.

Travel expenses for students with disabilities

The loan for students includes a set amount for transport costs (£303) – as a disabled student you can claim for travel expenses incurred over this amount if your disability means, for example, that you are unable to use public transport and must travel by taxi.

Social security benefits

Most full-time students are not entitled to benefits such as income support and housing benefit. However, such benefits can be available to students in vulnerable groups such as people with disabilities, but the situation is complicated. The people to put you in the picture are your Job Centre or Job Centre Plus, or Skill: the National Bureau for Students with Disabilities (see next page). Alternatively, phone the Benefits Enquiry line on 0800 882 200 or for minicom users 0800 243 355 (opening hours: 8.30a.m.–6.30p.m. Monday– Friday; 9a.m.–1p.m. Saturday).

Disability Living Allowance

The Disability Living Allowance is available to you as a student and provides funds on a weekly basis for those who need help with mobility, e.g. the cost of operating a wheelchair or the hire or purchase of a car. It also covers those who need care and assistance with any physical difficulties such as washing or eating, or continual supervision. The allowance will not affect your DSAs in any way. Again contact the National Bureau for Students with Disabilities.

Further information for students with disabilities

Contact the students' welfare officer at your university or college, or contact the students' union or local Citizens Advice Bureau.

The National Bureau for Students with Disabilities runs a special information and advice service, open Tuesday 11.30a.m.–1.30p.m. and Thursday 1.30p.m.–3.30p.m., tel: 0800 328 5050, and also publishes a number of useful leaflets (free to students) and books for disabled people, available from its website: www.skill.org.uk, or fax: 020 7450 0650, textphone: 0800 068 2422 or email: info@skill.org.uk.

Contact your local Job Centre/Job Centre Plus: contact details should be in your local telephone directory.

Royal National Institute of Blind People (RNIB), RNIB Education and Employment Network, 105 Judd Street, London WC1H 9NE, tel: 020 7388 1266 or helpline: 0303 123 9999, open Monday–Tuesday/Thursday–Friday 9a.m.–5p.m., Wednesday 9a.m.–4p.m. (messages can be left on the answerphone outside these hours), email: helpline@rnib.org.uk or website: www.rnib.org.uk.

Action on Hearing Loss (formerly Royal National Institute for Deaf People, RNID), 19–23 Featherstone Street, London EC1Y 8SL, tel: 0808 808 0123, textphone: 0808 808 9000, fax: 020 7296 8199, email: informationline@hearingloss.org.uk or website: www.actiononhearingloss.org.uk.

Bridging the Gap: A Guide to the Disabled Students' Allowances can be downloaded at www.direct.gov.uk/en/disabledpeople/educationandtraining/highereducation/dg_10034898.

Hardship funds

This is called the **Access to Learning Fund** in England; **Discretionary Funds** in Scotland; **Financial Contingency Fund** in Wales; and **Support Funds** in Northern Ireland.

Whatever the name, hardship funds are available in all parts of the UK, and at all universities. All four funds operate in much the same way – providing additional help to students who need extra financial support.

If you are in real financial difficulty, this is the source to tap. The fund is open to both full-time students and part-time students studying 50% of their time on a full-time course. It is there to help those facing particular financial hardship, those in need of emergency help for an unexpected financial crisis and those who are considering giving up their studies because of financial problems. Priority is given to students with children, mature students, those from low-income families, disabled students, students who have been in care, and students in their final year.

Payments are usually given as a grant, but they could be given as a short-term loan so make sure you have all the terms and conditions before you accept the payment.

You should apply as soon as trouble starts to loom. The fund is limited to the amount that is in the pot, so it is largely first come, first served. We have heard of institutions that have allocated most of their funds by the end of November in the academic year.

To apply for money from these funds you will need to apply to your college. Every institution will have a different procedure and different criteria for measuring your needs. You will probably have to fill in a form giving details of your financial situation. Most institutions will have somebody to help and advise you. They may even have a printed leaflet giving you details.

Funding is generally only given when all other avenues have been exhausted such as loans. The size of the financial pot is announced one year at a time. The pot for 2012–13 is £36m, slightly down from last year's £40m.

'Ask for help as soon as you realise you have a financial problem, as it takes at least four weeks to assess an Access to Learning Fund application. But in the end I got £200 – a lifesaver when you can't pay your rent.'
Fourth year, Astrophysics, UCL

Students from abroad

Unfortunately students from abroad cannot apply to the hardship funds. It is restricted to domestic students only, so overseas students are not eligible.

Hardship funds from universities and students' unions

Some institutions and also some students' unions have resources to help students in real financial difficulty. They all vary according to the institution, and they will pay out money for a variety of reasons. Funds are generally given when all official avenues are exhausted. Priority is often given to students who are suffering financially because of unforeseen circumstances such as a death in the family or illness. Sometimes small amounts are given to tide you over or to pay a pressing bill.

A point to note: increasingly, hardship payments are taking the form of an interest-free loan, which can be especially useful if your grant or loan cheque doesn't arrive on time, but it does mean you will need to pay the money back. Universities and students unions may also offer help to students from abroad.

Other sources of finance

While government maintenance grants and university bursaries are the main forms of debt-free funding, that is not the end of the story. There are other sources you can tap including trusts, charitable awards, and scholarships, bursaries and grants from other sources.

A reality or a vain hope?

You'd be right to be a little sceptical. If there were a prodigious number of organisations all eager to hand out money to students, you wouldn't have seen so many student demonstrations highlighting their financial plight or stories in the press about the difficulties students face. But there are a surprising number of educational charities, trust funds and foundations, professional bodies and benevolent funds in this country that offer financial help to students. Amounts from

£12 to £5,000 and everything in between are available. This may take the form of a scholarship or charitable award. One directory of grant-making trusts we consulted listed over 1,500 organisations under the broad heading of 'Education'.

But before you get too excited and think you've found the route to a crock of gold, be aware that when you start sifting through the many restrictions by which trusts generally have to abide, you soon realise there are relatively few – if any – where you meet their exact requirements. Having said that it's definitely worth checking out whether there are any sources which could work for you.

Scholarships

Scholarships provide money while you study. This can be for your full course, just a year or a one-off payment. They can be for a specific purpose such as travel, to fund some special area of research, to study abroad, to support a specific talent.

They are usually, though not always, given by an institution (this could be your university, a professional institute or a charitable trust) rather than by individual companies.

Competition is keen. Awards can be made on the grounds of academic achievement, ability in a specific area such as music or sport or because of need. Whatever the criteria, they are not going to come your way without considerable effort and often disappointment, so be prepared. Nobody gives money away easily.

University and college scholarships

Some universities and colleges are endowed by generous benefactors and can award scholarships and bursaries to selected students who meet the required criteria.

Usually an institution will have a very mixed bag of awards that bear very little relation to its academic strengths and interests. Most establishments don't give many awards, and competition in the past has been keen. But with the advent of increasing fees, universities are looking to provide many more scholarships and bursaries for students to offset the high cost of university education and attract more applicants.

Many of the university scholarships on offer have a subject or location condition attached, which does considerably limit those eligible to apply – perhaps you have to live within the boundary of a certain village. By and large they favour the traditional subjects such as engineering, history, geography, languages, law and the sciences but others are for the distinctly unusual, such as cultural criticism studies, paper science, rural studies, retail studies, leisure, town planning, textiles – and a great deal in between.

Scholarships for excellence

These are usually awarded for excellent A level results, other exams, or competitive exams held by the university, or you may find these scholarships are based on your university performance. These scholarships are not always income related. To give you an idea, here are a few examples of academic excellence awards:

- ► Birmingham Business School offers a Business Management and Marketing award of £1,000 for one year
- ► BP Undergraduate Mechanical Engineering Scholarship: this is worth £2,000 per annum and is given for academic excellence and examination results
- ► Manchester University Andrews Scholarship offers up to £5,000 to a civil or mechanical engineer from the Manchester area. It's given for excellence and financial need
- ► Southampton offers 10 scholarships of £1,000 to new students studying pharmacology or zoology based on qualifications and another 10 scholarships of £1,000 for outstanding performance in the first or second year
- ► Southampton Fashion and Marketing Scholarships worth £500 are given on a first come first served basis
- ► St Andrews University: introduced in 2012, this new academic excellence scholarship programme offers scholarships of £5,000 to its top 100 students at the end of their first year. This is open to all students irrespective of domicile or nationality. Go to www.st-andrews.ac.uk and key in 'undergraduate scholarships' for information
- ► UCL offer £3,000 faculty undergraduate scholarships.

See your university website for excellence scholarships and ask your university how to apply.

Slightly different are the Wellcome Trust Scholarships – these offer hands-on experience of research during the summer vacations to promising students, with a stipend of £180 a week (£190 in London).

Sports scholarships

Sports scholarships and bursaries are becoming increasingly common. These cover areas such as rugby, cricket, netball and even golf. A sports scholarship is a boon for any student who plays in a national team and needs to take time out for coaching to train for an international event. You can be studying any subject to get a sports scholarship.

Music or choral awards

A number of universities and colleges give music or choral awards. Many of these are from old foundations and the award may include a commitment to take part in services in the college chapel or local church or cathedral.

Geographical boundary awards

There are also awards with geographical restrictions. For example, students at Bangor University might get an award of £300 if they live in Criccieth or, better still £1,500 if they were born in one of the counties of Anglesey, Conwy or Gwynedd, while Exeter University students whose parents have resided in Devon for at least three years could be in line for a scholarship ranging from £12 to £80 per annum.

Travel awards

Your university may also give travel awards to undertake special projects during the vacation, for certain subjects. Ask your university for details of possible awards, and check their prospectus or website. For more information and some specific examples of this, see page 167.

Awards for foreign students

Overseas students are eligible to apply for many of the awards offered by universities. In some universities, there are awards specifically for foreign students, for example: engineering and applied sciences at Aston (£1,500–£3,000); law at City University London (£1,500 approximately); and a number of scholarships at Edinburgh for students from Japan, Malaysia, Singapore, Thailand and the US. For further information, contact the British Council or British Embassy in your own country, the British Council in the UK (www. britishcouncil.org) or the university where you will be studying.

How much would a scholarship be worth?

Awards vary tremendously: some are given annually for the length of the course, others are a one-off payment. The highest award we found for undergraduates was £5,000 while the lowest we found, at Exeter, was £12 – this is because the foundation was created in the 19th century when £12 was a lot of money, and its status cannot be changed.

Getting a scholarship

Scholarship distribution methods differ from institution to institution and of course according to the terms of the foundation. Your best option is to contact each institution to find out their particular method.

You should look at your university website. You can also try the Complete University Guide bursary grids at www. thecompleteuniversityguide.co.uk.

Scholarships from professional institutions

Some professional institutions give scholarships, some don't. The engineering institutions are among the most generous. Awards are made to students studying accredited degree courses.

Institution of Engineering and Technology (IET)
There is a range of IET undergraduate scholarships available up to £3,000 per annum plus free IET membership. To be eligible you must plan to study an IET accredited MEng or BEng degree course and expect to achieve 300 UCAS points.

IET grants are also available to those starting the second, third or final year of study and expecting to achieve a 2:1.

There is also an IET Power Academy scholarships of £2,200 per annum (for full details see Chapter 5).

The Baroness Platt of Writtle Award of £1,000 is given to final year students on an IET-accredited course.

The E3 Academy sponsorship for students starting an electrical energy engineering degree at the universities of Nottingham or Newcastle includes a bursary of £2,500 plus paid work placement (pay approximately £1,250 per month). See Chapter 5 for more details or visit www.e3academy.org.

The UK Electronics Skills Foundation bursary includes £1,500 plus summer work placements for students studying BEng or MEng degrees in electronics or electronic engineering at accredited universities. See www.ukesf.org/scholarship-scheme for more details.

To find out more about the IET and for details of awards, how to apply, and a list of accredited degree courses see the website: www. theiet.org/ambition.

Institution of Civil Engineers (ICE)

The Quest undergraduate scholarship offers up to £2,000 per annum plus a summer work experience placement with a leading company. There are currently over 250 Quest scholars studying in the UK.

The ICE technician scholarship is worth £1,500. For more information see the website: www.ice.org.uk/quest.

Institution of Mechanical Engineers (IMechE)

There are a variety of scholarships such as:

▶ IMechE Undergraduate Scholarships
▶ IMechE AMEC Undergraduate Scholarships
▶ IMechE Land Rover Spen King Sustainability Award.

Scholarships are worth £1,000 per annum during study periods. Applications are made online. For the application form and the relevant dates see www.IMechE.org/about-us/scholarships.

Whitworth Scholarships are available for undergraduate degree-level courses (including MEng and MSc) valued at £4,500 per annum (full-time study) and £3,000 per annum (part-time study). Even though the scholarships are handled by the IMechE, scholarships are available to outstanding engineers of any discipline who have undertaken a two-year hands-on engineering apprenticeship before commencing their undergraduate studies.

Go to www.whitworthscholarships.org.uk for more details of these awards and how to apply.

Institute of Marine Engineering, Science and Technology (IMarEST)

Up to four scholarships of £1,000 are awarded each year to undergraduate students attending approved, accredited courses leading to registration for chartered status – Chartered Engineer (CEng), Chartered Marine Scientist (CMarSci) or Chartered Marine Technologist (CMarTech)

Go to www.imarest.org for more information and details on how to apply.

Charitable awards

It would take a book several times the size of this one to list all of the charities and trusts which give help to students. For example the *Educational Grants Directory* lists more than 1,600 charities that between them give away more than £60 million a year – and this is by no means an exhaustive list. Help given covers fees, maintenance, books, equipment, travel either to and from your institution or abroad, special sports activities, child-minding and special projects. They all vary in what they will offer, and to whom.

Typical examples of why money might be given could be:

▶ a parent is suddenly made redundant and can't continue to finance your course fees

▶ a student who has been paying their way through their course through part-time work but feels they need to give up their job to concentrate on that final two-month push.

The difference between a scholarship and a charitable award is, again, very indistinct, and you could say there is no difference at all, as charitable awards can often be scholarships.

Charitable awards are always paid out by a charitable organisation, which must abide by the terms and conditions of the original endowment. So, however good and reasonable your case may be, if the money has to be paid out to a student from Gloucester studying chemistry, it is no good being an arts student from Leeds. To claim an award, both you and your financial predicament must fit the charity's help profile.

Often the payments available are small (under £100) but they can be more substantial – say £1,000 or more. It is unlikely that you will be able to fund your higher education through a charitable trust: it could be done, but don't depend on it. Payouts generally cover the cost of books or equipment – but if they are substantial they could cover fees or maintenance. They can be one-off payments, or given each year for the duration of your course.

Many charities won't consider you until you have tried all the usual channels available to students, such as loans and access funds, and they tend to give help towards the end of a course rather than at the beginning.

Trusts and charities fall largely into four major groups.

1. **Need.** For example charities for people with disabilities. Well-known organisations such as the RNIB and Action on Hearing Loss (formerly RNID) fall into this category, along with less familiar organisations such as the Shaftesbury Society and Scope.
2. **Subject.** This includes charities that will give help to students studying certain subjects. For example, the Honourable Society of Gray's Inn is just one of a number of charities helping would-be lawyers; and there are quite a few charitable organisations set up to help those studying medicine, for example the Charity of Miss Alice Gertrude Hewitt, which helps some 40 students aged under 25.
3. **Parents' occupation.** This can be a great source of additional income. If one of your parents is an airline pilot, artist, banker, barrister, coal-miner, gardener, in the clergy, in the precious metals industry, you name it, there

could be some help. Some trusts stipulate that your parent should be dead, but fortunately not all.

4. **Geographical location.** Where you study and also where you live can really make a difference. Take, for example, the lucky students living in the parishes of Patrington and Rimswell in East Yorkshire, in Oadby in the Midlands or in Yeovil in Somerset – they could be in line for help towards books, fees, living expenses or travel abroad. There are literally hundreds of these trusts covering many areas of the country.

Places to look for scholarships and charitable awards

Schools

Most schools will have a list of local charities that offer help to students and so you should ask for help to find out more about the scholarships and charitable awards which may be available to you. The fact that you have been to the school could be a condition of receiving a grant. Also try your primary school. It is a good idea to find out whether such scholarships, grants and charitable awards are available before you send off your UCAS application, as these sometimes stipulate a certain HE establishment.

Local authority

Your local authority should also have details of any local charities offering help to students in higher education.

EGS

The Educational Grants Service (EGS), which is part of Family Action, is an independent organisation that offers a range of services providing information on funding for those in post-16 education in England. EGS specialises in funding from charitable trusts, it administers funds from over 30 educational trusts and maintains a database of some 120 trusts and charities that assist students and will carry out an online search for you. You will need to put your information into their online database, which will then match you to the charities and trusts that are most likely to help you. The criteria for eligibility are set by the individual trusts and charities or by the people who bequeathed the legacy, not EGS, and are therefore extremely diverse. For further assistance you can phone the EGS helpline on 020 7241 7459, open Tuesday, Wednesday and Thursday 2p.m.–4p.m. or check out their website: www.family-action.org.uk.

Lone parents

Family Action also delivers the Horizons Education Fund which supports lone parents needing help to study. Further details can be found at www.family-action.org.uk/educationalgrantsprogramme.

Search the net

The web has a fund of information on sources for finding charities and trusts. Type 'educational grants charities and trusts' into your favourite search engine and follow the leads. Refugees could strike lucky if they visit www.lasa.org.uk. Another helpful site is https://nationalcareersservice.direct.gov.uk/. One excellent site to try is Scholarship Search UK, website: www.scholarship-search.org.uk.

One of the best websites we found is University Grants UK. Just click on the subject you want to study or click on the location; website: www.unigrants.co.uk.

Parents' employers

A surprising number of companies and large employers have special trusts set up to help with the education of their employees' or former employees' children. Typical examples are:

- ▶ the National Police Fund, which helps the children of people who are serving in or have served in the police force
- ▶ the Royal Medical Benevolent Fund, which helps the children of medical graduates
- ▶ the Dain Fund Charities Committee (contact the British Medical Association – www.bma.org.uk), which helps the children of registered members of the medical profession
- ▶ the Royal Pinner School Foundation, which helps the children of sales representatives.

What to read

▶ *Educational Grants Directory*, published by the Directory of Social Change.

▶ *The Grants Register*, published by Palgrave Macmillan, lists help mostly offered to postgraduates. See the website: www.palgrave.com.

▶ *Directory of Grant Making Trusts*, published by the Charities Aid Foundation, lists some 2500 grant-making trusts.

▶ *The Charities Digest*, published by Waterlow Information Services.

Most of these publications should be in your local library. Make that your first port of call as they are expensive. Otherwise see Amazon.co.uk.

Applying to charitable trusts

You can apply to more than one charity but blanket application is not advisable. Limit your applications to organisations that are really likely to give you funds. Most trusts have an application deadline. This is usually given along with the general information in the trusts and grants directories. Check out each entry carefully – they are all different.

Trusts are not the answer for a fast financial fix. Like all bodies, they tend to move exceedingly slowly. Your case will be scrutinised along with many others, so it could be months before you get an answer.

There are no set rules for application. What one charitable trust wants, another won't. The usual procedure is as follows.

▶ Put together a list of suitable charities by consulting either EGS or directories in the library.

▶ Find out exactly what each charity is offering and whether you meet their criteria.

- ▶ Check if there is a final entry date for applications.
- ▶ Write a brief note to your selected charities, explaining your need and asking for an application form.
- ▶ Fill in the application form. Make sure your answers are clear, concise and truthful. You may be questioned on them later. Bear the trust's criteria in mind.
- ▶ Photocopy the completed form before you send it back.
- ▶ Wait patiently. These things can take many weeks to process.

i advice note

Before making an application to a charity, it is important to be clear in your own mind exactly what kind of student they are likely to help, and what kind of financial assistance you are after, otherwise you could be wasting both your time and theirs.

What are your chances of success?

Your chances of getting a big pay-out are slim, although the odds are certainly better than the likelihood of winning the national lottery. Competition is fierce. This year, EGS has received 780 written applications, and completed 68,749 online trust fund searches. EGS includes the Educational Grants programme which administers over 30 educational trusts, providing small grants principally to families and individuals on low incomes, particularly those living on benefits. Funds are not available for items already covered by statutory funding, repayment of loans, childcare costs or daily living expenses.

i advice note

If you get help from a charity it shouldn't affect any other grants or bursaries. Charitable awards, scholarships and sponsorships are not generally taken into consideration when calculating your funding package.

Overseas students and those wanting to study abroad

It is very difficult to find trusts willing to fund overseas students who are already studying in the UK, and EGS cannot assist students wishing to study outside the UK. However, there are trusts that give funding for travel, and these should be contacted directly. EGS could be a good starting point. Scholarship search databases can be found on www.educationuk.org and www.hotcoursesabroad.com.

For more information, check out the following websites:

► www.britishcouncil.org.uk
► www.family-action.org.uk
► www.ukcisa.org.uk
► www.refugeecouncil.org.uk
► www.educationaction.org
► www.hotcoursesabroad.com
► www.educationuk.org
► www.direct.gov.uk
► www.refugeeaccess.info.

Additional funding from the devolved regions

Welsh students

Welsh students should try the Welsh Assembly, which offers bursaries to Welsh-born students attending Welsh universities.

Scottish students

The Carnegie Trust for the Universities of Scotland provides:

► financial assistance to students of Scottish birth or who have at least one parent born in Scotland or who have completed at least two years' secondary education in Scotland and who want to attend a Scottish university to study for a first degree
► vacation scholarships to enable undergraduates at Scottish universities to undertake a research project during the long vacation

▶ scholarships for three years' postgraduate research at a university in the UK, usually in Scotland.

Contact the Carnegie Trust for the Universities of Scotland, Andrew Carnegie House, Pittencrief Street, Dunfermline, Fife KY12 8AW, tel: 01383 724 990, fax: 01383 749 799, email: jgray@carnegie-trust. org or website: www.carnegie-trust.org.

The Student Awards Agency for Scotland (SAAS) maintains a register of educational endowments of Scottish trusts, many of which are local and open only to Scottish-born students who want to attend Scottish universities and colleges. The agency will search the register on behalf of any student who submits an enquiry form. Forms are available from SAAS, Gyleview House, 3 Redheughs Rigg, South Gyle, Edinburgh EH12 9HH, tel: 0131 476 8212, email: saas.geu@scotland.gsi.gov.uk or website: www.saas.gov.uk.

Competitions!!

Why not? The world is full of competition addicts. There are magazines devoted solely to the topic, steering readers to the next give-away bonanza. Whole families eat crazy diets just to get the labels off the right tins and jars.

People do win – holidays in exotic places, new cars, toasters, DVD players, washing machines, computers, £3,000 to spend on groceries and cuddly toys. It's always worth having a go, especially if it only means filling in a form online or texting a code to a phone number.

While most competitions cannot be seen as a serious means of raising finance, if it's a competition set by your university with prizes for excellence, in a subject area you know well, you're in with a real chance – and winning could be a useful addition to your CV.

A little icing on the cake is perhaps the best you can hope for, and even that is quite a hope. But don't dismiss competitions altogether.

For something less food-centric

There are competitions more in keeping with your academic studies. BP, for example, sponsors an essay competition to strengthen their ties with Imperial College London. Boring – did I hear you say? I don't think that's what William, a first-year undergraduate at Imperial, thought when he won first prize of £1,000, nor indeed the two runners-up who pocketed £750 each.

Do people win?

Another happy competition winner is Rachel, a first-year Drama and Theatre Studies student at Royal Holloway University.

She has won the £100 *Cut the Cost of Uni* prize draw. When she heard, she emailed us, 'Oh my goodness you have no idea how much this has absolutely made my month.'

To a student like Rachel who faces a final university debt of £30,000 you might think a few quid was nothing, but as she excitedly told us, 'It will mean a few extras next term. Strangely it seems to mean more than my escalating debt.'

Rachel is a deserving case. She is on a very tight budget and chose to share a room this year. 'It has saved me about £1,000 on accommodation and it is not as bad as I thought it would be.'

She gives photographic and graphic design classes to other students to earn extra money, and works as a freelance face-painter at children's parties. She has just bought a portable printer, with the idea of dropping a picture of each child into their party bags. 'I thought it would give me a USP.'

Is it worth it?

The litmus test with any competition has to be: 'Is it worth it?' Look at the hassle involved, the cost, the time factor, the number of cans of baked beans or cat food you have got to get through and what are the odds, do you really want the prize – and above all, read the small print carefully before you make a decision. The drawback with any competition is that the winner takes all, and the also-rans get nothing. Still, it doesn't hurt to keep your eyes open.

Try typing 'competitions' into your favourite search engine and see what you find 'Win £3,000, win an iPad2, win a relaxing spa day, win a Safari trip for two, win. . .' I hope you do! Best of luck!

5 Sponsorship: what it is and where to find it

Sponsorship is like a gold mine. A stash of money is lying hidden out there somewhere, it is just a matter of knowing where to look and digging it out. There is no better source of debt-free funding for university than sponsorship.

This chapter is a brief guide to sponsorship:

- ► what it is
- ► how to get it
- ► what to expect when you do
- ► what sponsorship can mean in terms of funding your studies as well as your future employment prospects
- ► the industries that commonly offer sponsorship
- ► the universities most likely to offer it
- ► how you can go about getting it yourself
- ► work experience and internships: an integral part of the sponsorship story.

Sponsors and sponsorship

Sponsorship is probably the best and most comprehensive way of raising extra finance to help you through higher education. It gives you money during term time and paid work during the holidays. It may also give you help with, or even pay in full, your fees. Added to that, it will not affect any grants or bursaries you are given.

You've heard of big companies sponsoring events such as the London Marathon, the FA Cup and cricket test matches – it means that they back the event with money. In the same way, an organisation could sponsor you through university.

Sponsorship can be given at various points during your degree study. For a full course it could be given after your first year of study or after an industrial placement. For the final study year, it will generally be given if you have accepted a job with the sponsor.

Sponsorship tends to be given to degree and HND students and comes largely from manufacturing and production companies, with engineering and related disciplines being the most sponsored subject. Those studying finance, business and IT subjects can be lucky, but many sponsors spread the net wider and just look for ability. The National Grid, for example, will consider students from a wide range of degree disciplines.

Typical sponsors include:

▶ employers: mainly large manufacturing, production and engineering companies, banks, accountancy firms etc.
▶ the three armed forces
▶ the Ministry of Defence: Defence Engineering and Science Group (DESG) www.desg.mod.uk
▶ professional bodies, e.g. IMechE
▶ universities, on behalf of employers.

Sponsorship can radically change your final debt and help your career prospects, so what's it worth?

Looking at it purely in cash terms, sponsorship could provide a £1,500–£3,500 annual bursary (the average is approximately £2,000) given during academic study. For manufacturing and production students it could be higher. The armed forces give higher rates still, but they have a different kind of arrangement.

You should expect to receive a monthly salary of £1,200–£1,600 from your sponsor during work periods, and remember most sponsorships offer at least eight weeks' work during the summer vacation. Remember also salaries are generally age-related, so a third-year student would earn appreciably more than a pre-university student.

Now add in the following extra benefits:

► invaluable work experience

► additional skills and training

► probably a secure job when you graduate. Companies tend to employ the students they have sponsored.

And you have the full picture. You can't put a price tag on experience but you can on the rest.

Table 5.1. Cut your debt: with annual sponsorship

Typical annual sponsorship	£4,500
Bursary	£1,500–£3,500
Vacation salary	£2,400–£3,200
Industrial placement salary	£15,000 plus

Although this may seem like an ideal solution to your funding problems, you have to face the fact that sponsorship is getting harder and harder to find in the current economic climate and competition is keen.

Why do companies offer sponsorship?

The reasons most often given by employers are:

► to have access to high-quality students before they graduate, with the hope of future employment

► to assess students over a longer period as potential employees

► to develop a student's skills and have an input into their training

► to publicise the company as a potential employer among other students.

How does sponsorship work?

There are no set rules – every company devises its own scheme. But in principle it works like this. As a sponsored student you would get training, work experience and financial help while at college – to varying extents, depending on the company scheme. You might be asked to work for a whole year in the company either before or during your course; or you might only be expected to work during the summer vacations.

In return, the sponsor gets the opportunity to develop close ties with 'a potentially good employee' and influence your development. There is generally no commitment on either side to employment after the sponsorship. However, since the company has invested a considerable amount of money in you as a student, it is unlikely not to offer you a job.

'Because I had sponsorship, had worked for a year before university and had a Saturday job, I didn't need a maintenance loan – but I took it out anyway, and put it in a good building society account, just in case I wanted to go on to do further study. As it was, my sponsor offered me a job that's too good to turn down, so I won't need it, but it was nice to have that security cushion there. I haven't checked it out yet, but I think the loan has actually made me money; at least it hasn't cost me anything, which has to be good.'

Third-year student

What sponsorship would mean

There are many types of sponsorship. Generally, it will include a bursary given while you are studying and paid work experience, which is usually at the going rate for somebody of your age. In financial terms, it would probably mean that you would be around £40–£80 a week better off than your contemporaries during term time, or better still have nearly £1,000 less debt each term with guaranteed work for at least eight weeks during the summer. But it's not just about money – the work experience and training are valuable assets, too.

Sponsorships and your other financial support

Any scholarship or sponsorship you receive should not be included when calculating how much loan, grant and university bursary you can have. Money earned during vacations is also not included. So a normal sponsorship shouldn't affect any other financial support you receive.

You do not have to pay tax on a bursary, but if your annual earned income is above the tax threshold (currently £8,105 for 2012–13) you would have to pay tax. So in theory, a year's placement would not be tax-free. However, since your year's work probably falls into two tax years you may find you pay very little or no tax at all.

Applying for sponsorship

There are various ways to apply for sponsorship.

► You apply to a company that offers sponsorships (these are generally offered to students doing specific subjects).
► You are offered sponsorship after a period of work experience.
► Your university has contacts with employers.

Subjects that most often attract sponsorship

Engineering outstrips any other subject, with the largest number of sponsorships being found in the manufacturing and production sector. However, there are opportunities for civil engineers in the construction industry. Many employers look for subjects with a close link to their own business activities. Good examples are food science, quantity surveying and polymer technology. So if you feel you are studying a degree relevant to a company's business drop them a line – it is worth a try.

A few organisations, especially in the financial sector, will sponsor people on any degree course, but you have to have an interest in finance.

Sponsorship schemes for students studying engineering or science

The Power Academy

The Power Academy is an engineering scholarship fund launched in 2004 for students studying an Institution of Engineering and Technology (IET) accredited degree course at a partner university.

It is backed by the IET, seven universities and 13 companies in the power industry. There are over 60 scholarships available in 2012 to students studying a full time course at the following universities: Bath, Cardiff, Imperial College London, Manchester, Queen's Belfast, Southampton and Strathclyde.

What the sponsorship offers:

► annual bursary of £2,200
► payment towards university fees for students who take up employment with their sponsors
► a books and software allowance of £220
► paid summer vacation work: at least eight weeks with earnings of approximately £2,307 (based on full-time salary of £15,000)
► mentors from industry partners
► free membership of the IET
► annual seminar for all Academy sponsored students.

The Power Academy was set up because there is a shortage of good electrical and power engineering graduates coming out of universities and the industry could be facing a crisis. It is anticipated that 25% of the power industry's current engineering workforce will retire over the next 15 years, and there are not enough good people around to fill the vacancies. So it looks as if there could be some good jobs available in the future.

The companies involved include: ABB, Atkins Power, CCFE, CE Electricity UK, EA Technology, National Grid, Northern Ireland Electricity, Npower (RWE PowerGroup), Rolls-Royce, Scottish Power, Scottish and Southern Energy, Siemens and Western Power Distribution.

To find out more, check with your university website or visit www. theiet.org/poweracademy.

Table 5.2. Cut the cost of uni: with the Power Academy

Annual bursary	£2,200
Book grant	£220
Eight weeks' work	£2,307 approx.
Total each year	£4,727

E3 Academy: sponsorship worth £5,000 a year

The E3 Academy is a sponsorship programme open to students applying to study for an undergraduate degree at the Schools of Electrical and Electronic Engineering at the universities of Bristol, Nottingham and Newcastle.

Benefits include:

- £2,500 per annum bursary for each year of study
- eight weeks' summer vacation work experience/training
- minimum rate of pay £1,250 per month
- attendance at the E3 Academy Summer School
- industrial mentor
- endorsement by the IET
- potential for a first-class career with your sponsor on graduation
- contribution towards fees if you take up employment with your sponsoring company.

Sponsoring companies taking part: Converteam, Siemens, Cummins, Control Techniques, Parker SSD, Edwards.

To find out more visit www.ncl.ac.uk.

Table 5.3. Cut your debt: with a four-year sponsorship from the E3 Academy

Bursary	£10,000
Salary	£10,000
Total	£20,000

Plus help with fees if you join your sponsor.

Ministry of Defence sponsorship schemes

The Ministry of Defence (MoD) offers two sponsorship schemes, the Defence Engineering and Science Group (DESG) scheme and the Defence Technical Undergraduate Scheme (DTUS) scheme.

DESG Sponsorship Scheme. The aim of the DESG student sponsorship scheme is to help you explore the variety of careers available in the Ministry of Defence (MoD) while gaining valuable work experience. There is no commitment to work for the MoD on graduation under this scheme but obviously they hope that you will join them – and most students do. The scheme offers:

▶ a bursary of £1,500 per annum which is given while studying

▶ 10 weeks' guaranteed paid work experience at an MoD establishment in the UK during summer vacations (pay is £3,528 based on a full-time salary of £18,350 and reviewed each year)

▶ work placements which are designed to give valuable experience to engineers and scientists, so expect a challenging project that will make a real difference to the team you are working with

▶ a mentor assigned to all students who will help them select summer placements and provide advice on professional development.

The scheme is open to those studying an approved engineering or science degree in a UK university and who are likely to achieve a 2:2 degree or better.

Visit www.mod.uk/DefenceInternet/AboutDefence/WhatWeDo/ScienceandTechnology/DESG/for more information. Applications for new students start in the autumn for the following summer sponsorships.

DTUS Sponsorship Scheme. The Defence Technical Undergraduate Scheme (DTUS) is a university sponsorship programme for students studying an approved science or engineering degree who want to join one of the armed services or the Engineering and Science branch of the MoD Civil Service as technical officers after they graduate. You would be sponsored by the MoD to study an IEng (Incorporated Engineering) or CEng (Chartered Engineering) accredited engineering degree course.

To be eligible you must show a commitment to join the DESG Graduate Scheme and give a minimum of three years' service within one of the armed services or the MoD Civil Service. Also you must be studying an approved DTUS science or engineering degree at one of the following universities: Aston, Birmingham, Loughborough, Southampton, Newcastle, Northumbria, Oxford or Cambridge.

The scheme offers:

- a bursary of £4,000 per year paid for each year of university study
- a guaranteed 10 week paid summer placement at a MoD establishment unless undertaking a DTUS expedition (pay approximately £3,528 with a salary review in August)
- £33 per day for support unit activities. These will include one night per week during term-time for formal dinners, social occasions, sports and adventurous training exercises.

Visit www.mod.uk/DefenceInternet/AboutDefence/ WhatWeDo/ScienceandTechnology/DESG/ DefenceTechnicalUndergraduateScheme.htm for more information.

See also sponsorship schemes in the armed services which cover wider career opportunities on page 146.

Other sponsorship schemes to consider

The **UK Electronics Skills Foundation** which is for students studying for a BEng or MEng in electronics or electronic engineering. It offers an annual bursary of £1,500 plus paid summer work placements; see the website: www.ukesf.org/scholarship-scheme.

The **National Instruments NI Engineering Scholarship Programme** which offers a £1,500 award for the second year of study, plus an NI mentor, and a 1-year paid industrial placement. See the website: http://uk.ni.com/careers/scholarship.

BP offers a range of scholarships, sponsorships and internship awards. For example:

- final year awards, given to a range of engineering disciplines, includes a £5,000 cash award and entry to a BP Assessment Centre

- the BP Scholarship award, includes £2,000 given for one year; you can re-apply each year
- BP internship awards, which offer a £2,000 scholarship plus internship salary.

See the careers section at www.bp.com or look on university websites.

GCHQ has a studentship sponsorship scheme, although their website stresses that what they have on offer is continually changing. For the summer of 2012 they offered the following which will give you an idea:

- summer placement: nine to 12 weeks over summer, plus subsequent sponsorship of final year
- two-year summer placement: placements and sponsorship for last two years of degree
- industrial placement year: 51 weeks plus subsequent sponsorship.

For more information see the website: www.gchq-careers.co.uk.

Coming soon: new for 2013

The Institute of Engineering and Technology will launch a new excellence scholarship scheme for students on IET accredited courses. Three As at A level and you win.

The above schemes are just a taster of the many sponsorships that are available. Research is the answer – on the internet, through your university, through professional institutions and bodies and not just before you start your studies. Determination should open up useful links and hopefully opportunities.

The financial sector: accountancy firms

If anyone can spot a good financial deal for students it should be an aspiring accountant. Here are four training possibilities for the financially astute to ponder offered by the UK's leading accountancy firms: KPMG, PricewaterhouseCoopers (PWC), Ernst & Young and Deloitte.

KPMG: a new radical approach to study

If you are prepared to take a radical new approach to studying for a degree with guaranteed employment at the end and absolutely no debts to face then take a look at the new KPMG school leavers' degree programme. There can be no better way of not just cutting but eliminating university costs.

Launching this scheme on their website, KPMG say, 'We believe that our school leavers' programme is a compelling alternative to pursuing a traditional university route.'

It certainly is if you:

▶ want to avoid any debt and still get a good degree

▶ want to be an accountant

▶ are happy to make that career choice at 18 and sign up for the next six years

▶ are prepared to be part of the world of work and to work hard.

Tick all these boxes, and it would seem you are onto a winner.

This is how it works.

▶ You join KPMG, one of the UK's largest accountancy firms straight from school and are put on their school leavers' programme.

▶ You are on a starting salary of £20k (in London).

▶ You join one of the firm's audit teams.

▶ You study for an accountancy degree at a top university – Durham, Birmingham or Exeter – for set periods of time each year on a specially devised course.

▶ Your degree will take four years to complete.

▶ You will then study for a further two years to become a fully qualified chartered accountant with the ICAEW (Institute of Chartered

Accountants in England and Wales) or ICAS (Institute of Chartered Accountants of Scotland).

► All your fees at university and accommodation cost while studying will be paid by KPMG, potentially a saving of up to £70,000.

► Your salary over the six-year period is likely to rise substantially.

► You will have no worries about finding a job when you graduate.

► You will miss out on the long student vacations.

► Only high achieving A level students will be accepted: entry requirements ABB at A levels, plus a B in GCSE Maths and in English Language (or equivalent).

Limited to 100 school leavers a year, the competition is likely to be keen. However some students on the Student Room website (www.thestudentroom.co.uk) had their doubts.

► If you are 100% sure you want to do accounting then take the KPMG route …

► If you fail your exams with KPMG you'll be left with nothing but work experience …

► A degree is much more flexible …

Students join the KPMG scheme each September. Visit www2. kpmgcareers.co.uk for more information.

PricewaterhouseCoopers (PwC)

PwC offers the Flying Start Programme which has been going since 2002. Run in partnership with Newcastle University and the Henley Business School, it enables students to put classroom theory into commercial practice. Here's what it offers:

► it's a four-year degree programme

► students study for a BA (Hons) Business, Accounting and Finance degree at Newcastle University or BA (Hons) in Business and Accounting at the Henley Business school, Reading University

► in Years 2, 3 and 4 of the degree students undertake periods of paid work experience at PwC: 16 weeks if studying at Newcastle and 20 weeks at Henley

► salary is paid during periods of work experience: £20,000 pro rata

- with a good performance and a minimum 2:1 degree you can expect to be offered employment
- the combined approach means you will be well on your way to qualifying as a Chartered Accountant.

Visit the website: www.pwc.co.uk.

Ernst & Young

While the Ernst & Young and Deloitte (below) schemes would possibly fit better in our chapter on earning while you study (Chapter 7) we have included them here so you can compare what's on offer from the top accountancy firms.

This Ernst & Young scheme focuses more on paid internships that take place largely in your penultimate and final year. It offers:

- a 12-month placement as part of your degree
- a six-week internship in your penultimate year
- an 11-week global exchange offered to exceptional performers looking for international experience. Only 50 lucky students selected. Flights and accommodation paid for.

Successful placements could lead to job offers. Visit the website: www. ey.com/uk/en/careers.

Deloitte

Deloitte has a completely different approach and again it is quite radical. Their scholars scheme provides a unique opportunity to combine travel during a gap year with paid business work experience. The scheme offers:

- a 30-week paid placement starting the August/September after you finish your A levels
- a £1,500 bursary to go travelling after your placement
- a £1,500 bursary during each academic year
- a minimum of four weeks' paid work experience placement each academic year

- ► exemption from first interview stage if you apply to join as a graduate
- ► around 40 scholar placements.

Visit the website: http://careers.deloitte.com.

The sponsorship process

When you can get sponsorships

You can get sponsorship at various points in your studies:

- ► after A levels or BTEC for a full degree or HND course
- ► after a gap year spent with a company between A levels and higher education
- ► after your first year of study
- ► after a successful period of work experience or an industrial placement year for your final year of study.

While sponsorships are still given to A level students for their full 3–4 years of academic study, more and more companies are choosing to sponsor students later in their degree course when they have established a commitment to the subject. Work placements and sponsorships are now considered to be one of the best graduate recruitment tools by large employers.

'The sponsorship market has changed. Companies have certainly cut back on numbers and many offer only a final-year sponsorship, but I think it has reached its trough. Many of the smaller organisations that only want one or two sponsorship students are now going straight to the universities of their choice and asking for who they want. This is largely to avoid having to deal with the thousands of applications which advertising in our publication would engender. There are some good sponsorships around which are well worth going after.'

University Schools Liaison Officer, IMechE

When to apply for sponsorship

Full degree course sponsorship. Some companies offer sponsorship for your full degree course. Applications for these schemes should be made early in your final school year, and at least by the time you submit your UCAS form. Ask when applying to universities if sponsorship is available.

Second-year degree course sponsorship. Some sponsors like to see a commitment to your course before offering sponsorship. Applications should be made early in your first year at university. Ask your head of department for likely sponsors.

Final-year degree course sponsorship. Increasingly, employers are offering sponsorship to students for just the final year of their degree course. Often this will be offered after a successful industrial placement year or summer vacation placement. Employers offering sponsorship at this stage will expect students to agree to join them after graduation.

The competition for sponsorship is phenomenal. All sponsors say that applications outstrip sponsorships available, and it is getting worse – so get in early. The earlier you apply the better. Applications for full course sponsorship should have been made by the time you submit your UCAS form.

What is a sponsor looking for?

A straw poll of sponsors suggested that sponsors favour students with:

▶ good A level (or equivalent) grades
▶ maturity
▶ potential
▶ ambition
▶ evident team skills
▶ sense of humour
▶ hard-working attitude
▶ ability to get a good second-class degree
▶ interest in their degree topic

- ability to assimilate information and learn quickly
- a spark that sets you apart from the rest
- business awareness
- interpersonal skills.

i **advice note**

- Make sure any literature you are reading on sponsorship is up to date – school and college careers libraries may not yet have the current information.
- Look at your contract in detail and, above all, check the small print.
- Question your sponsor; they will respect you for that.

What to expect when applying for sponsorship

The application form

These are more likely to be online than paper forms, and you need to think carefully when filling them in because you only get one chance. Mess it up and your application will go no further.

Employers are – quite naturally – looking for the brightest and best students to sponsor; they want to have the pick of the potential high-flyers at an early stage. If you are applying for sponsorship before you start university, you may only have GCSE results, possibly some AS level results and a head teacher's report to show what you are capable of. This can be tough on those who wake up academically after GCSE or who really excel only in their one chosen subject. But good employers are more aware than you might expect; selection is not made on academic qualifications alone.

Sponsors are looking for signs of those additional qualities needed to succeed in your chosen career, such as leadership potential, the ability to grasp ideas quickly and to work in a team. They want ambitious, innovative people with get-up-and-go, who can think for themselves and get things done. So if your GCSE grades slipped a bit – or, as one student we interviewed put it, 'you look like Mr Average on paper' – think through what else you have been doing. Playing in the football or hockey team, helping out at the local club, hiking across Europe, getting a pop group together ... it could help to redress the balance. Remember, the application form is the first weeding-out process and you are up against stiff competition. This is no time for false modesty – you've got to sell yourself for all you're worth.

The interview
Interviews vary enormously. Some companies give a full-scale assessment with psychometric testing and tricky questioning and watch how you respond to certain situations. Others are much more laid back and go for a straight interview. Whatever the process, if you are an A level student it will probably be something quite new to you. Don't worry. The company will be fully aware of this and will not ask you to do something you are not capable of. Remember, too, that your competitors will be in much the same position. Still, you shouldn't expect an easy time at an interview. This is often the crucial decider.

UCAS and sponsorship
Many sponsors ask for expected UCAS points of around 300. Generally, you have to apply to UCAS and for sponsorship at the same time, which makes for complications. However, both sides are aware of this, so a system has been worked out. First, you should discover whether a sponsor you are interested in requires you to gain a place on a particular course – if so, you should name that course on your UCAS form.

However, it could happen that an employer you had not originally been very interested in offers you a sponsorship with the proviso that you gain a place on a course not named in your selection on your application form. While UCAS does not generally allow students to make alterations to their original application, in the case of sponsorship they usually relax this rule.

Deferred entry
Another complication is whether you want deferred entry or not. If you get sponsorship, your sponsor may require you to do a pre-degree

year in industry, but at application time you may not know this. If in doubt, apply for the current year. It is always easier to ask a university to defer your entry rather than bring it forward. On some courses, especially popular courses such as law, deferment may be more difficult to arrange.

Scott's sponsorship story

If you want to really cut the cost of university this is the way to do it. Scott, a first-year Engineering Science student at Oxford, not only has his fees and maintenance paid, he is actually making money out of going to university.

Scott, now 18, was thumbing through his local newspaper, the *Westmoreland Gazette*, when he saw an advert offering university sponsorship to two students.

The company was Gilkes of Kendal, specialists in hydropower systems and pumping application engineering. At the time he was applying for a university place and so contacted Gilkes. He knew of them since the ski slope he used was next door.

A tough interview, but he was offered sponsorship for his full four-year degree course plus employment when he graduated.

This was the deal.

► The company would pay his fees: currently £3,290.

► He would be paid £550 a month for each year, £6,600 per annum reviewed annually.

► He would work in the company for eight weeks during his summer vacation. No extra salary since he is already receiving £550 a month.

► On graduating he would be offered a job within the company and would be contracted to stay with them for three years.

- By the end of this period he could expect to become a chartered engineer.

- On graduating, if he wanted to break the employment side of the contract and work for another company he (or hopefully his new employer) would have to repay his sponsorship.

- In the unlikely situation that the company could not offer him a job he would not have to pay the money back.

What is his sponsorship worth? Using today's figures the total is about £39,560, but fees and maintenance will increase over the next four years so it will be worth considerably more in the future.

For example, if Scott was starting his course this September, with the increase in fees, his sponsorship would be worth at least £62,400. (With fees escalating to £9,000 there is no guarantee his sponsor would have paid his fees in full.) As well as financial gain, Scott will also receive invaluable work experience.

In addition to his sponsorship, Scott takes out a student maintenance loan which he puts straight into an ISA paying 3.3%. This is a higher rate of interest than the inflation rate which the loan accumulates while he is studying (as a pre-2012 student he pays a different rate of interest to new students). So he is actually making money from his course. He also has a holiday job as a lifeguard at a local caravan site pool; he works up to 20 hours a week for £6.82 per hour. In a good week that's £136.40 per week.

His major outgoings are as follows:

- accommodation plus food: £1,200 a term
- an expensive hobby: Scott has joined his college go karting team, costing him approximately £1,000 per annum.

Of his sponsorship Scott says, 'Sponsored students work on "live" projects at Gilkes during their work experience periods, so what we do is useful to the company. Through work experience you see the relevance your academic work has in the real world of work which certainly helps with your studies.'

Table 5.4. Cut the cost of uni: Scott's sponsorship deal

Income	For one year	Approximate figure over four years
Fees	£3,290	£13,160
Bursary	£6,600	£26,400
Earnings	£2,728	£10,912
Total	£12,618	£50,472
Major outgoings		
Fees	-£3,290	-£13,160
Accommodation/food	-£3,600	-£14,400
Go karting	-£1,000	-£4,000
Remaining income	£4,728	£18,912

Income/outgoings for four years in Table 5.4 above are just to give a guide. Scott's fees/accommodation over the four years of his degree are likely to increase, so too would his bursary and earnings.

Possible cutbacks

The increase in fees is giving generous sponsors reason to think. The Power Academy (see page 126), who in the past have paid the fees of sponsored students, are currently offering a contribution towards fees and only if the student joins the sponsoring company on graduation. Others may follow suit.

Work experience

Students gain amazing experience during placements – but you should make sure it is the right experience for you. It is important not to be so mesmerised by the bursary money that you don't consider what the company offering sponsorship does and whether it can provide experience that will help your career. Experience is a major asset on your CV and could help lift you out of the pile of hopefuls. The downside to a sponsorship is that during your degree all your work experience will be in one company and, because of this, it can shape the direction of your future career. When you go for your interview, ask about the experience and training you can expect and the skills you will acquire.

Terms and conditions

Check the details and watch out for the wriggle room. Remember sponsorship is a contract. You do not want to sign up to something that you will regret later. Ask your head of department/teacher if still at school, or parents for their opinion.

Time spent with your sponsor

Some sponsors demand you spend a year working with them either during your course or for a gap year before university. Others give you the choice. Most stipulate summer vacation work of six to eight weeks. Students often ask for more and many do Easter vacation work as well. Engineering firms are generally more demanding and the sponsorship is more likely to be geared to a sandwich course, so you could be looking at a full year in industry plus two summer vacation placements.

Planned vacation work

Some companies will hold special vacation planning sessions. These are usually during the Easter vacation and can last anything up to a week. During these sessions, you might plan with your sponsor how you want to spend your summer vacation time.

Sponsors occasionally allow their sponsored students to gain experience in other companies during vacations, as they feel that it will help to broaden their mind and knowledge. But most are loath to do so, for obvious reasons.

Obligations

You are not obliged to join your sponsoring company after graduating, unless it says so in your contract. Equally, your sponsor is not obliged to offer you a job. But there is no doubt that companies are taking a tougher stand these days, and seeking value for money from their sponsorships, for example:

▶ some companies will stop your bursary payment for the final year if you don't agree to join them
▶ a few companies demand reimbursement of their sponsorship money if you don't join them. You would have been informed of this before you agreed to a sponsorship – it will be mentioned in the contract detail
▶ some companies only give sponsorship for the final year after a job offer has been accepted.

Losing sponsorship: what it could mean

Terminating sponsorship

Sponsorship is a legal contract. Look at the terms carefully. Most agreements will have a clause that allows the employer to withdraw if your academic performance is unsatisfactory. The loss of a sponsorship would probably scupper your debt-free university plans and could plunge you deeper into debt. There may be other clauses you should watch out for.

Academic performance

If you fail the odd exam, you're probably all right, but if your end-of-year results are so bad that you have to repeat the year, you may find that your sponsor is no longer interested.

You've chosen the wrong course

It can happen that you choose a course in something that you may never have studied before, and after a term or so you discover that you and the subject just don't get along together.

A sponsorship is not a life sentence, and neither is a degree course. Talk first to your college tutor. It may be just one aspect of the course you don't like. Then talk to your sponsor. You will probably be able to change your degree course, but it may be more difficult – or impossible – for your sponsor to put you on an appropriate sponsorship scheme.

This is not a good situation to be in. A change of heart can be an expensive business. A sponsor could demand repayment and so could your university. Be sure before making a move. But if you are sure you want to change, the sooner you speak up the better, before too much money is wasted.

How to choose a sponsor

'If you have a choice, be practical – go for the cash' is one student's advice on selecting a sponsor. Certainly cash is something to bear in mind, but there are many other factors to consider such as the following.

- ► Compare salaries for work experience and bursaries: the plus on one side might cancel out the minus on the other.
- ► Check out the training for engineers: is the training accredited by the appropriate institution? And the experience: is it a well-organised programme of development or are you just another pair of hands?
- ► Talk to students on the scheme: find out about projects undertaken; how many sponsored students joined the company as graduates?
- ► Where would you be located?
- ► Do they provide accommodation if away from home?
- ► Are there opportunities to gain experience abroad?
- ► Finally, ask yourself: is it the kind of company where you would want to make your career?

In theory you shouldn't let sponsorship sway what course you decide to study. First, decide on the course that best suits you. You're going to spend at least three solid years – and possibly more – studying, so make sure you're going to enjoy it, otherwise the results could be at best disappointing and at worst disastrous. Not an easy choice if an employer is offering to pay your bills.

! **it's a fact**

Median starting salary paid to graduates in 2012 is expected to rise to £26,000 after remaining unchanged at £25,000 per annum for three years. Source: *AGR Graduate Recruitment Survey 2012 – Winter Review*.

Typical sponsors are large firms with 1,000–9,000 employees.
Source: *ASET*.

Where and how to look for sponsors

Universities and sponsorship

If you are accepted on to a course either conditionally or unconditionally, ask the course director if they know of any sponsoring companies, as many universities have a list of potential sponsors. Some students find that they are automatically offered sponsors to apply to and some courses are actually sponsored by employers and the sponsors are involved in the selection procedure. College prospectuses/websites may give you some guidance on this.

A number of universities advertise courses which may be sponsored in *Engineering Opportunities* – available at www.imeche.org/libraries/volunteer_Resources/Engineering_Opportunities.

The University of Manchester hosts a special site which lists many major companies offering sponsorship; these include AMEC Construction, Balfour Beatty Construction, Bovis, Costain, Faber Maunsell, Frazer Nash, Mott MacDonald and many more. Check out www.careers.manchester.ac.uk/students.

👍 **top tip**

Always ask about sponsorship – they could say no but they might say yes.

Not all sponsors advertise

If you look down the list of sponsors in most sponsorship books, you will be surprised by how many large companies appear not to offer sponsorship or work experience. Yet in fact they do. Many companies just don't bother to advertise – the requests flood in anyway. Others have special relationships with selected schools or universities. Some have just not thought of the idea. So just because a company doesn't advertise sponsorship, that shouldn't stop you from asking.

> ### *i* advice note
>
> Unlucky in securing sponsorship? Try the back door. When you're looking for a summer vacation job, seek out companies that you feel could be interested in sponsoring your particular skills. You may be lucky, and there's no harm in asking.

Don't forget the smaller companies

If you're thinking in terms of your CV, we admit that a well-known name will carry more weight than a smaller company. But with a smaller, little-known company there is less competition. Perhaps more importantly, you are likely to be treated as an individual. You may well be the only sponsored student they have and you can develop your own training and experience package. Of course, if they have no experience of sponsored students, they may not know what you are capable of and what experience you should be getting. So you could find you have to stand up for yourself.

Local companies

It is always best to apply to a company that interests you. Nevertheless, some companies do prefer to take on local people. From their point of view, there is no accommodation problem when it comes to work experience, and statistics show that many students want to return to their home town to work when they complete their studies. So the company is more likely to keep the sponsored student as an employee.

The armed forces

The three armed forces offer generous sponsorships, which can cover fees and full living costs. But there is a service commitment involved which you should think very carefully about before taking it up. Debt-free study it may be but your career could be set for the next few years and maybe for the whole of your life.

There will be a number of interviews. They will test your ability, fitness and suitability for an armed forces life. It is not enough to be clever and academically gifted. It is competitive, and you may find the interviewing process tough, though fair. Remember they are interviewing you for a demanding career where people's lives can be on the line, not just a sponsorship. But if you are what they are looking for, and a service life would suit your temperament, it will certainly cut the cost of your university studies.

Army

There are a range of sponsorship opportunities available including an undergraduate bursary scheme for students on any degree course and a cadetship scheme for medical and dentistry students. A commitment to join the army for a period of service is expected. Visit the website: www.army.mod.uk/join.

Alternatively, you could join your local (university) officer training corps which is good fun, offers excellent sport and social activities, and at least 15 days a year at training camp. Attendance at meetings and camp is always paid. The daily rate for officer cadets is £39.90 (as of 2011). Pay is subject to hours of attendance. See the website: www.army.mod.uk/UOTC/5458.aspx for details and your local UOTC unit's current rates.

Royal Navy and Royal Marines

There are various opportunities for students and any degree is considered. Specific degree opportunities: engineering, medicine, dentistry, and all schemes include a service commitment. Visit the website: www.royalnavy.mod.uk/careers.

Royal Air Force

Any degree is considered, but there are specific requirements for medicine and dentistry. A service commitment is expected and students are encouraged to join either the University Air Squadron or university military support unit. Visit the website: www.raf.mod.uk/altitude/educationandcareers.

Science and engineering students should check the Defence Technology Undergraduate Scheme (DTUS) on page 128 for sponsorship opportunities.

Internships and work experience as a route to sponsorship

This is often the best route into sponsorship. If they like you they won't want to lose you. There are many internet sites offering internships and work experience. Here are a few for starters:

- ► www.milkround.com
- ► www.monster.co.uk
- ► www.studentjob.co.uk/internship
- ► www.targetjobs.co.uk/work-experience.

Just be careful that what you are offered provides **valuable** work experience as well as extra cash. Ask yourself the following question: Is this a company I would want to join on graduation? This is really important as an employment commitment is often a condition for sponsorship. And as sponsorship is not guaranteed ask also:

- ► is the experience I am getting providing useful skills?
- ► is it helping to further my academic knowledge?
- ► will I receive any training?
- ► will this experience add to my CV?

Always find out the length of internship/work experience as it varies from a summer vacation to a full year. And if money is important make sure you are being paid and it's not the other way round. If no payment is offered, make sure fees are not demanded and find out what expenses you might incur.

If an advert for an exciting 'internship' abroad says, 'The difference between volunteering and an internship is the mentorship and evaluation you receive', make sure you know exactly what you are signing up to because the word 'internship' has many meanings (especially on the internet).

So what's it worth? Even without sponsorship to follow, eight weeks of work could earn you £2,400–£3,400, so for a year you are looking at a salary of £15,000–£21,000.

Banks

The Bank of England offers Penultimate Year Internships of six to eight weeks. Pay is £65 per day, which is £325 per week, a total of £2,600 for eight weeks' internship.

Outstanding performance could lead to the offer to join as a graduate entrant. Projects will involve collecting and analysing data and working closely with economists and analysts.

Will sponsorship be good for my CV?

Yes, but with reservations – 73% of the companies we asked said sponsorship was a plus point. The others felt that it made little difference. What is important on your CV is the fact that you have been employed. As a careers adviser at the University of Bath told us, '. . . while sponsorship shows that you have been "selected", it is the work experience that would be seen as the important element on a CV.'

Of course, prospective employers will probably ask why you didn't join the company that sponsored you, so you will need to have a well-phrased answer. Most employers realise that a decision made at the age of 18 may not look so right when you are 22. It's always worth remembering that a would-be employer may write to your sponsor for a reference, so it's important to leave your sponsoring company on good terms.

What you can gain from sponsorship

- ▶ Money: probably an annual bursary plus good rates of pay when working.
- ▶ Training: most sponsorships will involve some form of training.
- ▶ Meaningful work experience.
- ▶ Guaranteed employment for the summer in an area that will assist you with your studies.
- ▶ Chance of future employment: but no guarantee.
- ▶ Help with final-year project work: possibly.
- ▶ Opportunity to gain first-hand knowledge of the working environment where you might possibly start your career.
- ▶ Understanding of what it means to work in industry.
- ▶ Chance to gain new skills.
- ▶ Plus point to put in your CV.
- ▶ Less debt or better still **no** student debt.

What you can lose

- ▶ Your holiday time is not your own. So, for example, you would not be able to spend the whole summer abroad going InterRailing.
- ▶ You have the chance to see only one industry or company during work experience.
- ▶ You make a career choice at 18 that may not be what you want at 21.
- ▶ You may be obliged to work for a company whether you want to or not because of a payback clause.
- ▶ You may be asked to work in locations that are not very appealing and possibly a long way from home.

For further information: who to contact

- ▶ Local employers that interest you: many employers prefer to sponsor local students.
- ▶ Don't forget the smaller companies. Some may never have thought of offering sponsorship before, so it can be a matter of making yourself sound like a good bet.

- ► Your course director.

- ► Your university or college may well have a list of sponsors who are interested in sponsoring students on your particular course.

- ► Black and Asian high-flyers can also try the Windsor Fellowship undergraduate personal and professional development programmes, which include summer work placements and community work. Application forms and further information can be downloaded from www. windsorfellowship.org/leadership.

- ► Consult the Year in Industry (YINI – see Chapter 7).

- ► Look at *Engineering Opportunities*, published by the IMechE on behalf of the engineering profession. It lists sponsors, universities with sponsored courses and companies offering industrial placements and internships. Available free from IMechE c/o Marketing & Communications Department, 1 Birdcage Walk, London SW1H 9JJ or email: education@ imeche.org.uk.

Sell yourself

Finding sponsorship can be very hard work. It means writing persuasive letters to employers, making phone calls and selling yourself in a way that you have never done before. Modesty won't win favours. But the prize if you do win can be life changing – literally. A career, incredible experience and to crown it all the difference between a debt of £70,000 or one of £7,000 hanging round your neck for many years to come.

6 Money-saving strategies

This chapter explores some money-saving strategies you can employ while you're at university. It looks at saving money by:

- ► living at home
- ► part-time study
- ► distance learning
- ► tips and ideas for budgeting
- ► finding deals to save you money.

The cost-saving way to study

First of all don't get locked into a study straitjacket. Just because all your classmates are taking the traditional 3–4 year full-time university route it doesn't mean it's the best, and it's certainly not the cheapest, way to study.

You should investigate and compare:

- ► two-year degree courses
- ► part-time study
- ► distance learning.

The fast-track course: a two-year degree

This is the new kid on the block. Untried and untested in most universities, cost-wise it looks very promising. A two-year degree costs approximately £35,000 (fees plus living); while a three-year degree costs approximately £53,000 (fees plus living).

What is more difficult to measure is:

- academic effectiveness
- pressure of work on students
- whether the students miss out on other university benefits like sport, drama, hobbies, social and academic development
- development of additional skills.

But how important are these?

There are some definite plus points:

- less debt as you save on a year's fees and a year's living expenses
- you enter the job market earlier
- you get on the career ladder sooner
- a more concentrated course suits some students
- the extra money in your pocket: possible earnings of up to £24,000 per annum while your contemporaries are still studying and racking up even more debt.

However, fast-tracking your studies has its opponents. Here are a few concerns that some employers brought up:

- no time for work experience
- no time to develop transferable skills
- lack of intellectual maturity
- half of AGR recruiters* had not heard of the two-year degree, while those that had were concerned heavy workloads would prevent development of skills.

*Source: *AGR Graduate Recruitment Survey 2012 – Winter Review.*

While the government and academia talk about the merits of two-year degrees, a number of universities have taken the plunge. This is how Northampton University's two-year fast-track degree works.

- Students follow the normal academic year, but it is an intensive course.
- They then take extra modules over part of the summer break.

- They have the normal Christmas and Easter breaks and an extra month's study during the summer.
- Selection for intensive courses is generally more rigorous since the pace is fast and you need to keep up.
- They graduate with a full honours degree.
- Students are eligible for all the student funding on offer.

Subjects currently offered:

- LLB (Hons) Law
- BA (Hons) Management
- BA (Hons) Marketing
- BA (Hons) Sport Development.

Fees for these courses are £8,500 per annum.

Staffordshire University offers a fast-track two-year BA (Hons) in Accounting and Finance. The course programme looks like this:

- first block: September–January
- second block: January–May
- third block: June–August.

While blocks one and two follow the same programme as for a three-year degree the third block is a mix of distance learning and face-to-face delivery. All the advantages listed above are applicable.

Other universities offering two-year degrees include:

- Buckingham University
- Greenwich School of Management
- London School of Commerce
- University of Plymouth.

Table 6.1. Cut the cost of uni: with a fast track two-year degree

Outgoings	Three-year degree	Two-year degree
Fees	£27,000	£18,000
Accommodation	£13,500	£9,000
Living expenses	£12,000	£8,000
Total	£52,500	£35,000
Saving per degree course		£17,500
Earnings instead of study Year 3		£24,000 approx.

Distance learning

Well tried and tested. If you want to live at home while you study but get a degree from a good university then you may find that distance learning is your best option. That way you can take the course of your choice but cut back on your expenses. Courses can be studied over a number of years thus spreading the cost.

Many of our top universities run excellent distance learning courses:

▶ University of Birmingham

▶ University of Wales

▶ University of London

▶ Sheffield Hallam University

▶ University of Sunderland

▶ Anglia Ruskin University.

And there are many more.

If you need help try RDI (Resources Development International), website: www.rdi.co.uk, tel: 0800 268 7737. The website carries details of funding available and a list of designated courses.

There are distance learning scholarships available – mostly for postgraduates.

Thrift Tips

Save on food

'Get to like pasta!'   *Fourth year, Psychology, Paisley*

'If each of your friends brings a potato, carrot or leek, you've got a great stew for next to nothing.'   *First year, Music, Huddersfield.*

'For the price of a sandwich you can buy a whole loaf, a packet of meat and even the mustard.'   *PhD English Literature, St Andrews*

'Find food nearing its sell-by date and being sold off cheaply, then freeze it.'   *First year, Social and Political Science, Cambridge*

Open University

If funding is proving to be a major issue you could always consider the Open University (OU), probably the best-known distance-learning organisation in the UK. More and more young people are choosing the OU study-at-home way. With 250,000 students enrolled, of which 190,272 are undergraduates, the OU is the UK's largest university, with a high reputation. Its partnership with the BBC has resulted in lectures moving from late night screening to prime time viewing – for example *Frozen Planet*. The OU provides around:

► 600 courses
► 70 subject areas
► 250 different qualifications ranging from certificates to foundation degrees to full undergraduate and postgraduate qualifications.

As with other institutions, the fees vary dependent upon your country of residence, so the cost for students in England is appreciably more than for those in other regions.

Table 6.2. Cost of bachelor's (honours) degrees with the OU if studying full time (120 credits)

England	£5,000 p.a.
Scotland	£1,610 p.a.
Wales	£1,610 p.a.
Northern Ireland	£1,610 p.a.
Outside the UK	£5,000 p.a.

The annual fee paid also reflects the intensity of your studies. A full degree at the OU in England costs £15,000 (360 credits) and £4,830 in the devolved regions.

Typically, most students study part time. A 60 credit module per year (50% of a full-time course) equates to fees in England of £2,500 per annum and £805 in the devolved regions.

If you study 30 credits a year (25% of a full-time course) it will cost £1,250 per annum in England and £405 in the devolved regions.

Over 71% of OU students are in full- or part-time employment during their studies which means they're earning as they're learning and not racking up huge debts.

Help with OU course funding is available

England. From 2012 students will be able to apply for a government student fee loan to pay their fees (see Chapter 8).

Wales. Fee and course grants are available for students from low-income families, tel: 01908 653 411. The Access to Learning Fund in England and the Contingency Fund in Wales may also be able to offer some help.

Northern Ireland. Fee grants are available for students from low-income families.

Scotland. Students from low-income households may benefit from a fee waiver covering the cost of fees or a £500 grant towards fees, depending on income.

Can't get a fee waiver or student fee loan?

Open an Open University student budget account (OUSBA) and pay your fees in monthly instalments or when it is convenient to you. For more information and the latest rates, see the website: www.open-university.co.uk.

Table 6.3. Cut the cost of uni: study at the Open University

Cost of course	Full time at university	OU England	OU devolved regions
Fees	£27,000	£15,000	£4,830
Living	£25,000	£0	£0
Total	£52,000	£15,000	£4,830

Part-time study

Studying part time is another way to save money as it not only allows you to work to earn money while you study but you also receive some funding to help you through. There are more than 500,000 students studying part time in the UK and with the current increase in fees this figure is likely to increase.

Fees for part-time study in England have increased to a maximum of £6,750 per annum (less if you are domiciled in Wales, Scotland or Northern Ireland) so what funding is available?

England. The bad news is that no fee grant is given for part-time study and no maintenance assistance is given either. However, under the new funding arrangements part-time students can apply for a tuition fee loan for the first time so you will not have to pay fees up front (see Chapter 8).

Wales, Northern Ireland and Scotland. Part-time students doing 50% or more of a full-time course can apply for an income-assessed grant towards fees and in some areas a course grant. See Table 6.4 overleaf.

Table 6.4. Grants and fee grants for part-time students

Course	Northern Ireland fee grant	Northern Ireland course grant (maximum)	Wales fee grant	Wales course grant (maximum)*	Scotland fee grant*
50–59% of the full-time course	£820	£265	£690	£1,125	Up to £500
60–74% of the full-time course	£985	£265	£820	£1,125	Up to £500
75%+ of the full-time course	£1,230	£265	£1,025	£1,125	Up to £500

*2011–12 figures
Grants and fees for part-time students are means-tested on income and depend on intensity of course.

If I run out of money will my university help with funding?

Most universities have hardship funds and will be sympathetic to part-time students in financial difficulties. See page 105 for more information.

Other ways to save money

Save by living at home

More and more students are choosing universities where they can continue to live at home because it is cheaper. If your timetable means you only have to attend university three days a week, this can be a possibility even if you live a long way from your university. We heard of someone commuting from London to Cambridge.

For some students, the idea of living at home would be unthinkable: going to university is all about gaining independence. But if that results in you having to abandon your course because of debt, then you could be back where you started – at home! It's worth thinking about.

How much would you save by living at home?

Ask your parents. It might cost you nothing!! Just think what you would save on rent, food, internet connections, utilities, TV. Aled, a third-year student at Glamorgan university (see case study below), puts his saving at £10,000–£12,000.

Living at home: Aled's story

Aled is a final year student at the University of Glamorgan studying Sport Management.

'It was primarily to save money that made me decide to live at home and go to a local university. Fees for me are just £1,400 per annum for which I get a fee loan, and with no accommodation costs it just seemed to make financial sense.'

Aled did look at other universities, in particular Bournemouth, but the course modules at Glamorgan suited him better. He says, 'The Bournemouth courses veered more towards coaching and physical education while Glamorgan looks at the business side.

'I thought at the start by not living in college I might miss out on campus life. But during my first year I spent a lot of time sleeping over at friends so I didn't miss out on the social side at all.'

Aled lives just over three miles from the university and he has a car which makes campus very 'easy and accessible'. He adds, 'I have friends that live some 20 miles away and they certainly are missing out on university life.

'My car is a major expense, but it is an essential. With insurance of £700 a year, petrol £35 per week, tax £180 a year, parking at university £1.10 per day, and maintenance the car must cost me around £2,700 a year. My parents give me around £600 per annum towards the costs.'

To help cover his living and social expenses Aled has taken out a student maintenance loan of £2,400 and has a weekend job at Wetherspoons (Friday and Saturday nights 6p.m.–3a.m.) which earns him around £6,000 per annum.

'I don't think my job impacts on my studies as chances are I would just chill out on a Friday/Saturday night or be out drinking,' he says. Despite that he spends £30 a week on socialising and another £30 a month on football and the gym.

Living at home is easy. He has a twin brother and the family generally eat together. As his mother works, and he tends to get home first, he will cook the evening meal – which he enjoys.

Aled expects to graduate to a debt of £12,000 and an overdraft of £1,000. But he won't find this difficult to pay off. He hopes to start his Army Officer Training soon after he graduates.

Save by budgeting

Probably the best money-saving strategy you can employ while at university is to make a budget for yourself and stick to it. The principles of budgeting are incredibly simple but putting them into practice is, for many people, incredibly hard. It is a matter of working out what your income and expenses are and making sure the latter don't exceed the former. It may sound rather boring, but it's a lot better than being in debt.

A step-by-step budgeting plan

1. Take a piece of paper and divide it into four columns (see Table 6.5 on the next page). On the left-hand side, write down your likely income sources and how much they will provide, for example:
    - ▸ maintenance grant
    - ▸ bursary
    - ▸ parental contribution
    - ▸ fee loan

- ▶ student loan
- ▶ sponsorship
- ▶ money earned from holiday job
- ▶ money earned from term-time job
- ▶ money from the Access to Learning Fund

Table 6.5. Student budgeting plan

Income		Outgoings	Predicted	Actual
Grant	£	Fees	£	£
Bursary	£	Rent/college board	£	£
Parental contribution	£	Gas	£	£
Fee loan	£	Electricity	£	£
Maintenance loan	£	Telephone	£	£
Sponsorship	£	Launderette/cleaning	£	£
Job	£	Food	£	£
University hardship fund	£	Fares – term time	£	£
Other	£	Fares – to college/home	£	£
		Car expenses	£	£
		Books/equipment	£	£
		TV licence	£	£
		Student rail/bus card	£	£
		Broadband	£	£
Total	£	Total	£	£
		Socialising	£	£
		Hobbies	£	£
		Entertainment	£	£
		Clothes	£	£
		Presents	£	£
		Holidays	£	£

2. In the second column, write down what your fixed expenses will be – things that you have to pay out – like rent, gas, electricity, telephone, food etc. Don't forget to include travel fares. Now total them up in the third column.

3. Subtract your fixed expenses from your income and you will see just how much you have, or haven't, got left over to spend. Draw a line under the list and below it list your incidental expenses – things like socialising, clothes, the cinema, hobbies, birthdays etc. This is your 'do without' list: the area where you can juggle your expenses to make ends meet.

4. Apportion what's left over to the things in this list, making sure you've got at least something left over for emergencies. Do the figures add up?

5. Having worked out your budget, use the final column on your budget sheet to fill in exactly how much your bills actually come to. In this way, you can keep a check on your outgoings and how accurate your predictions were and do something before the money runs out.

The trouble with budgeting, especially for students, is that money generally comes in at one time, often in large chunks at the beginning of a term, and your outgoings are needed at other times. When you work you will probably find it easiest to budget on a monthly basis, but as a student you may have to do it either termly or yearly, depending on how the money comes in. As your loan comes termly, it is often a good idea to get the money paid into your savings account and then transfer money over, perhaps every week or every month. This will help you budget and spend within your means.

Seems simple enough and logical on paper. But of course, it doesn't work quite as easily as that. There's always the unexpected. You can't get a job. Your car needs a new battery. People use more gas than expected. Did you really talk for that long on the phone?

Thrift Tips

'Take out a certain amount of money each week and keep it in a glass jar; then you can see it going down.'

Second year, English Language, Lancaster

'Save coppers and small change; you'll be surprised how much you save – providing, that is, you don't cheat.'

First year, Birmingham

Arrange to have your monthly statements sent to your term–time address to help you monitor your budget.

Save on travel home

The most popular means of transport for students is the train. Don't leave it to the end or beginning of term to buy your ticket: some of the best ticket deals are limited to a set number of passengers. And never pay full fare. For example, at the time of writing:

▶ London to Manchester peak times – return by train costs £296

▶ London to Manchester off-peak advance booking return with travel card costs £33

▶ typical special deal £12 one way

▶ cost saving: 90%.

Remember if you do have to stagger home/to university with your luggage using public transport, your costs may need to include taxi fares.

Thrift Tips

Forward planning can save you a fortune on travel costs

▶ Plan your trips home and book early – there are some fantastic bargains on trains and coaches.

▶ Coaches are generally cheaper than trains, but they take longer and the amount of luggage you can take with you is usually limited.

▶ Travel on Friday is generally more expensive; reductions are available if you book in advance.

Further information on travel

For National Express enquiries, call 0871 781 8181.

For trains, see website: www.nationalrail.co.uk or just put 'train fares' into your search engine.

Save money by living closer to home

If you can pick a university closer to home it will be a saving. If you live in Devon and are studying in Scotland you may not be coming home very often but your travel bill could be enormous. If home is Sheffield and you study somewhere close at hand like Leeds, it's a relatively cheap trip (£11 return approximately). But then again, you might be tempted to go home weekly, which over time would add up.

Many students told us that their parents might give them a lift at the beginning and end of the year when they have a lot of luggage. That would certainly help save on costs.

Megabus, Megatrain and student rail and coach cards

Before you do anything, check out Megatrain and Megabus travel. With or without a card, they could be the cheapest option. Travel is available to many of the UK's largest towns and cities for as little as £1 each way plus 50p booking fees – rather less than to cross London on the tube. See www.megatrain.com or www.megabus.com for more information.

Regular train and coach services offer student reductions, provided you buy their special student cards, which last for a year. One longish journey will more than cover the initial outlay.

A **16–25 Railcard** costs £28 (cheaper online) for a one-year card. It gives you a reduction of one-third off all rail fares. There are travel restrictions so check with the station before you travel for full details. Also check the internet for any reductions or special offers as internet-only promotions are sometimes available.

A **Young Person's Coachcard** costs £10 for a one-year card, and gives you a reduction of up to 30%.

i **advice note**

Restrictions on student cards can change, so always check what is being offered and when you can travel.

Look for special reductions: occasionally, the rail or coach companies will have special promotions such as half-price student cards or half-price fares. They may also give discounts on things like CDs or subscriptions to magazines. Also check out www.gobycoach.com, and look for travelcards with local bus companies.

London students

If you are aged 18 or over and enrolled at an HE college or university in London you are eligible for an 18+ student Oyster card which could save you 30% off the adult rate of travel on buses, trams and underground trains.

Save on travel abroad

There are a number of travel organisations that operate special schemes for students. In fact, you will find they are vying for the privilege of sending you off on your travels, often dropping the price in the process. If you decide to take the cheapest, make sure it is a reputable organisation and a member of the Association of British Travel Agents (ABTA). It's better to be safe than stranded.

If you are taking a gap year, or your institution has no travel office, try STA Travel, which is one of the biggest names in the student travel business. You can check them out on www.statravel.co.uk or call 0871 230 0040. If you prefer face-to-face contact, they have 43 branches in or close to universities throughout the UK.

Also big on the student travel scene is the International Student Travel Confederation (ISTC) with 500 offices in 120 countries (including 33 in the UK) and some 10 million students and youth travellers on the move. Their website (www.istc.org) is a must for any would-be adventurer. Make sure you have an International Student Identity Card (ISIC): it gives you an entry to an amazing range of around-the-world opportunities. See details below.

Make sure you join these key organisations before you set off.

ISIC

ISIC's £9 card offers you thousands of discounts in the UK and around the world – from high-street stores to hotels and hostels, weekend breaks, flights, buses, trains, restaurants, guidebooks, entertainment, attractions, museums, galleries, CDs to travel gear, gym memberships, software and eating out.

You can also get low-cost international calls and texts in over 100 countries, free voicemail and an international travel emergency helpline via the ISIConnect phone and SIM card. ISIC is available to all full-time students. See www.isic.org for details of where you can get your card, or pop in to STA Travel.

International Youth Travel Card (IYTC)

The IYTC costs £9, and if you are not a full-time student but are aged 26 or under, the IYTC is for you. It offers fantastic discounts and ISIConnect services. It is available through ISIC (see above) or STA Travel.

Youth Hostel Association (YHA)

It costs £9.95 to join, if you are under 26 years old, and the YHA (England and Wales) Ltd offers access to UK and international youth hostels. Changes made to membership rules a couple of years ago mean that you don't even have to be a member to use their youth hostels. Non-members just pay a £3 a night supplement, or £1.50 per night for under-18s. However, you do need a membership card to use all Hostelling International (HI) member hostels in other countries. An annual card is now down to £9.95. A two-year card costs £16.50 (if you are under 26). There are more than 4,000 HI Hostels across 80 countries and they all have assured standards for hygiene and safety. An annual card for those over 26 costs £15.95, but couples can buy a joint annual card for £22.95. To join the YHA, write to YHA, Trevelyan House, Dimple Road, Matlock, Derbyshire DE4 3YH, tel: 01629 592 700 or visit the website: www.yha.org.uk.

InterRail

InterRail gives you the flexibility to see Europe the way you want to – you can go where you like, when you like. Your InterRail pass gives you unlimited travel on the extensive network that covers over 30 European countries. Choose a one-country pass from £42 or a global pass from £147. It is available to European citizens and anyone who has been resident here for six months. Go to www.interrailnet. com for more information on the different passes available.

> ### *i* advice note
>
> The internet is a great source for cheap travel and excellent deals for students, but make sure you are dealing with a reputable firm.

Let your university help fund your travel aspirations

Many universities have travel funds and scholarships. They will not fund frivolous holidays, but might well help with serious trips to help with your study or a trip which benefits a community project.

Manchester University Alumni Association

A typical example is the Alumni Association fund at Manchester University. In 2012 the Alumni Association offered Global Impact Awards of £250 to help students bring practical or social benefits to a community overseas.

You could be eligible to receive a Global Impact Award if:

▶ you are a current undergraduate student not in your final year of study

▶ your trip will have a sustainable benefit to the community you are visiting in a social or practical manner

▶ your trip will benefit a marginalised or vulnerable group

▶ your trip will enhance your broader development.

Will they repeat this next year? Try www.yourmanchester.manchester. ac.uk.

Leeds University

The Leeds for Life Foundation Grants are normally provided to support travel during the summer vacation. Awards are given to support students undertaking enterprising travel normally overseas. The Foundation tends to favour candidates whose planned travels will contribute to their personal development through encounters with different cultures, or a contribution to projects designed to promote positive social or environmental aims.

Awards are normally around £400. See the website: http// Leedsforlife.leeds.ac.uk.

Lincoln College, Oxford

A limited number of travel grants of £100–£250 are available to support travel connected with undergraduate studies in general.

Linguistics students can apply for a £200 travel grant plus the above standard travel grant to put towards travel abroad. Visit the website for more details: www.linc.ox.ac.uk/Travel-Grants.

Save on phone and mobile bills

Certain 08 numbers (0844, 0845, 0870 and 0871, for example) masquerade as costing the same as local calls but may not be as cheap as you think, and may not be covered by any cost-saving phone deal you have in place either. Many mobile phone packages exclude freephone numbers such as 0800 and 0808, so you pay the going rate for calling these. To find the cheapest way to phone an 08 number, visit www.saynoto0870.com. It might give you an alternative local number, or show how your call can be routed in a different way.

Check out the latest mobile phone deals at moneysupermarket.com. Decide how much you use your phone, and find out whether your provider has good reception in your university area. Your mobile phone is where your social life probably begins. If you use Skype phone calls are free. For more on saving money on your mobile see page 43.

How to save on shopping

You can save 5%, 10%, 15%, even 40% off your shopping bill by looking out for the retailers giving student discounts such as:

- ► Accessorise
- ► Adobe
- ► Apple
- ► Arcadia
- ► Comet
- ► Gap
- ► Microsoft
- ► New Look

- Rymans
- and many, many more.

Make sure you have your NUS card always to hand – it's the quickest way to a discount.

Save with the help of the NUS extra card

The NUS extra card is the must-have, money-saving card for all students. Benefits include:

- exclusive discounts on all the things you want or want to do – food, accommodation, drink, going out, mobiles, sports, films, insurance and banking, technology – you name it
- savings when you travel.

On average this card saves a student £500 a year, and costs only £11.00 (look at local union offers before buying). You can apply online and the card will be delivered within 7 days.

Don't make a move without it! Visit the website: www.nus.org.uk.

Thrift Tips

... for drinkers

'Organise parties at home and get others to bring the drink.'
Second year, Journalism, Film and Media, Cardiff

'Drink cider rather than beer – it's cheaper and takes less to get you drunk.'
Fourth year, Biochemistry, Oxford

'Become teetotal.'   *Third year, Design, Wolverhampton*

'Learn to drink slowly.'   *Third year, English, Wolverhampton*

'Reduce your cuppa expenditure – buy a kettle, a cafetière, and a thermos flask.'   *Third year, Geography, Oxford*

A dozen budget saving dos and don'ts from students

- ► Voucher clip: whenever you see a voucher tear it out and save it, you never know when it will come in handy.
- ► Bursaries/grants/hardship funds: know your rights and make sure you get what you are due.
- ► Cook together: it's cheaper.
- ► Check out money-saving sites on the internet, such as groupon. co.uk, livingsocial.com, moneysupermarket.com, vouchercodes. co.uk and voucherseeker.co.uk
- ► Always ask for a student discount: you may be lucky.
- ► Go North: accommodation is cheaper.
- ► Shop late, when date-sensitive food is discounted.
- ► Print on both sides of the paper.
- ► Shop on cashback sites.
- ► Rent out that extra box room (ideally to a small tenant).
- ► Skype: it's free.
- ► Never shop on an empty stomach.

Save on hiring

Renting fully furnished doesn't always mean fully equipped. You may find what is provided is just not adequate. Many students told *Cut the Cost of Uni* that the best way to save was to cook in bulk and then freeze the rest. If everyone in the house does the same you may find your freezer is overflowing. The answer could be to hire a second freezer.

It is better to rent than buy since maintenance is generally included and as one astute student living in a rough area told us, 'TVs have a way of walking'.

Typical prices for standard products:

- Dishwasher (saves the 'whose turn is it to wash up?' rows): £3 per week
- Freezer: £2.50 per week
- Fridge/freezer: £3.50 per week
- Washing machine: £3 per week
- Tumble dryer (remember, who pays the electricity bill?): £2.50–£3 per week
- Washer dryer: £4 per week
- TV 26"–27": £3 per week
- TV £32": £6 per week
- TV 40": £9 per week
- TV 50": £10.50 per week.

Save on broadband

Don't just look at the headline cost. Will your broadband provider offer enough Mbps and download capacity to serve the whole house?

☑ **what to look for when choosing broadband**

- Free set-up.
- Free first three months.
- Minimum length of contract: you may not be there for more than nine months.
- Is line rental included?
- What else is included: do you want it to cover your TV?

7 Earning while you study

Earning while learning is becoming an increasingly important part of the funding package. Many students depend on finding a job to fill their funding black hole. Without it, their debt just keeps on mounting. In this chapter we'll look at the options you have for earning money while you study:

▶ part-time jobs during term time
▶ holiday work
▶ paid work placements
▶ internships
▶ taking a gap year
▶ working while studying abroad.

We'll also look at some tricks and tips from students on some more unusual (but still legal!) ways to earn money.

Part-time work

Most students do it. When they realise that their funding won't actually stretch as far as they thought, usually by the second term, they start to look. There is always a scramble for part-time jobs during term time, so if you need extra cash move fast. For students who work, average part-time earnings account for about a quarter of their weekly expenditure when accommodation is included.

Table 7.1. Average weekly earnings and expenditure

Accommodation	£81.70
Living	£120.24
Total	£201.94
Earnings	-£48.46
Deficit	£153. 48

The average figure above is less than 8 hours' work at the minimum wage of £6.19. Many students earn and work a lot more.

'I work in the uni bar for 20 hrs a week and earn £500 a month.'
Second year, Politics, Royal Holloway

'One hour's work every night for £9 caring for an elderly couple. It means I never get an early night so I can get very tired.' Total £63 a week.
Third year, Dentistry, Dundee

'As a steward at rugby matches I earn £70 a day, but only when there's a match on in Cardiff.'
First year, International Wildlife Biology, Glamorgan

'During the Easter and Summer vacations I work three days a week, 6 hours a day at Mencap earning £8 per hour.' Total £144 per week.
Third year, English Literature, Bristol

Most universities and colleges allow students to work during term time; in fact, many universities have set up job shops, so you could say they are actively encouraging it. But most suggest a limit on the number of hours you work during term – generally 15 hours a week, although some say 10–12 hours and others up to 16. The university students' union is a great source of work, providing job opportunities in its shops and bars.

The number of students who actually work during term time varies between universities. Most universities just don't know. However, the percentage at some universities is very high. Manchester university estimates that over 50% of their students work during term time, and recommends working no more than 15 hours a week.

How much can you earn?

Jobs offered through the university website/job shops will pay at least the minimum wage of £6.19 if aged 21 or over, £4.98 if aged 18–20 (figures from 2012). Fortunately many jobs pay more. Internships/industrial placements are generally the best payers as pay is linked to the salary graduates would earn, around £15,000 per annum (see page 183).

How Danielle cuts her debt

She works 8 hours on Saturday in a cash and carry for
£6.16 per hour = £49.28 per week
'It hasn't impacted on my studies yet but then I'm in my first year. This may change.'
Business Management, Sussex

Danielle's annual budget

Accommodation: £2,940
Living: £2,100
Job: £1,921
Deficit: £3,199

The tutor's view
'When it comes to work, academic staff attitudes vary from the positive to the negative. Obviously, they would like it if students didn't have to work, but are realistic, especially with the introduction of fees. If you want to encourage students from diverse financial backgrounds, then you have got to be prepared to let them work.'
Co-ordinator of Student WorkPlace, University of Manchester job shop

The students' view
*'Part-time work teaches you discipline and keeps you from being in the
bar every night.'*
Third year, Sociology, De Montfort

*'I work 15 hours Friday and Saturday nights. I don't think it impacts on my
studies as I'd either "chill" on Friday/Saturday nights or go out drinking.'*
Third year, Sports Management, Glamorgan

*'Two 4 hour shifts a week, gives me £50 a week. A bit less time for
coursework but I cope with it well and it gives me a bit more to spend.'*
Fourth year, Biomedical Science, Dundee

Getting a part-time job certainly can make a difference to your
finances as the table below shows. Rents are fairly stable and most
students seem to be keeping their cost of living down.

Table 7.2. Student's average weekly budget

Town/city	Average weekly rent	Average total weekly expenditure incl. rent	Average weekly earnings term time	Average hours worked per week during term	Extra cash needed per week
Birmingham	£62.74	£199	£74.81	10.9	£124.19
Brighton	£112.87	£225	£38.95	6.3	£186.05
Bristol	£83.76	£189	£35.68	6.2	£153.32
Cambridge	£91.82	£209	£26.04	6.6	£182.96
Cardiff	£79.68	£205	£57.85	10.0	£147.15
Dundee	£67.71	£175	£101.97	15.9	£73.03
Edinburgh	£87.81	£200	£33.80	5.6	£166.20
Glasgow	£87.72	£183	£81.40	11.3	£101.60
Leeds	£86.72	£206	£65.87	10.7	£140.13
Leicester	£83.66	£208	£30.85	4.3	£177.15
Liverpool	£69.69	£182	£47.72	9.3	£134.28
Manchester	£80.74	£217	£55.72	8.1	£161.28

Newcastle	£64.68	£194	£64.07	11.3	£129.93
Nottingham	£70.75	£219	£40.56	7.4	£178.44
Oxford	£96.85	£222	£49.42	7.4	£172.58
Plymouth	£85.74	£181	£47.86	7.3	£133.14
Portsmouth	£74.76	£197	£48.22	6.7	£148.78
Reading	£88.74	£216	£47.00	5.8	£169
York	£77.68	£210	£21.23	4.1	£188.77

Source: NatWest Student Living Index Survey 2010.

How Natasha cuts her debt

Working at her university bar for 20 hours a week – the maximum hours allowed at her university – and earning the minimum wage. As she is only 18 that's just £4.98 per hour = £99.60 a week.
First year, Politics, Dundee

Natasha's annual budget

Accommodation: £4,469
Living: £1,560
Earnings: £3,884
Deficit: £2,145

Going against the trend are Oxford and Cambridge, where many (but not all) colleges actively forbid or strongly discourage students from working during term time, except perhaps if they work in the student bar. Since the Oxbridge term is just eight weeks long and, as one lecturer pointed out, 'very intensive weeks at that', perhaps the colleges have a point.

What students do

Students seeking evening or weekend work during term time will probably find it easier in a large city than in a small town. London students should fare better than most – which is just as well, since they are among the most financially stretched. You are most likely to find work in bars, restaurants or general catering, dispatch-riding (you'll need your own wheels and a fearless mentality!), pizza delivery, office or domestic cleaning, babysitting, market research, office (temporary work), hotels, and of course, shops and supermarkets.

Table 7.3. Typical student jobs and rates of pay

Type of work	How job was found	Pay per hour	University
Horticulture manual work	Family	£6.30	Lancaster
Museum steward	Web	£8.00	St Andrews
Charity mugger	Friend	£7.00	UWE
University ambassador	University	£7.00	Keele
Bike mechanic	Asked	£5.35	Huddersfield
Front of house for arts venue	Friend	£6.47	Aberdeen
TK Maxx	Advert	£6.06	Dundee
Website designer	Offer to students	£10.00	Oxford
Nightclub	Job centre	£5.50	Essex
National Trust admin	Temp agency	£6.50	Lancaster
Laundry	Placement another dept	£6.06	Dundee
Sports Stadium	Advert in programme	£6.10	Glamorgan
Gymnastics coach	Asked	£150 per month	Dundee
Basketball coach	Interview	£10.00	Wolverhampton
Holiday cottage cleaner	Friend	£8.00	Falmouth
Guitar teacher	Worked in music shop	£15–20 per hour	Dundee

Party planner	[Not known]	£5.00 approx.	Hull
Gigs	Word of mouth	£5–£100	Dundee
Piano teacher	Advertised in local school	£10 approx.	Queen's Belfast
University bar	Asked	£9	Royal Holloway
High street retailer	Shop window	£6.11	Stranmillis UC
Ironing	Imagination	£5.00 approx.	De Montfort
Secret shopper	Job shop	£5.50–£11	Hertfordshire

Holiday work

The best jobs are internships and work experience. Both should provide skills and experience vital for your future and CV. Pay (which is mostly given) can be excellent as it is often relative to your degree skills (see page 183 for more details).

If money is the motive then returning home and looking for a job would be the most cost-effective move, especially if your parents don't charge for food and accommodation and there is no travel involved.

☀ cash crisis

Meeting up with old school friends can eat into your earnings, especially if they are not students, and don't always look for the cheapest places to go.

Help from your university

If you are wanting to spend the vacation at university then your university job shop is the place to turn (see page 182).

Working abroad

Summer camps especially in America, Canada, Australia New Zealand and many other places provide students with a fun experience and new skills. You probably won't come home with a fortune but it won't cost you either. It will also look good on your CV. Try BUNAC, website: www.bunac.org.

How Jessica cut her debt

'This year I am in France working at a school earning €800 a month as part of my mandatory year abroad. Last year I worked at the university cafés part-time earning £200 a month.'
Third year, Combined Arts course, Durham

Volunteering

A money-making solution it is not, whether in the UK or overseas. It may even cost you money so could increase your overall debt. However, volunteering is a fascinating/laudable thing to do, and it could provide you with valuable additional skills much appreciated by employers so it could pay off in the long term. It is possibly a better option for a gap year project or even a sabbatical, and again looks good on the CV. (See university travel awards on page 167.)

Aspiring entrepreneur

Facebook, Google, Microsoft, just three of the great entrepreneurial ideas that sprang from a university bedsit. There are many others such as Dell, Yahoo, *Time Magazine* for example. These are the megastars and their success stories are well documented. But the trend goes on.

Take the two Cambridge graduates with massive debts of £50,000 to pay off who decided to rent out their faces as advertising hoardings to companies at £400 a day. A simple but effective idea which takes face painting to a new high and has earned the enterprising duo over £25,000 in little more than six months. What started as a bit of a joke is now going global, well international. Will they hit the mega bucks?

Many universities have what they call business incubators, organisations to help students get started – Bristol University has Basecamp and London Metropolitan has Hatchery for example. These incubators are places to nurture entrepreneurial ideas that may well turn into businesses.

Sadly, we are not all budding Zuckerbergs. Most students are only too glad to find some way of earning a little extra cash to help them through university. Here are a few ideas we heard about from students.

Ideas from student mini entrepreneurs

- ▶ eBay is often a good place to start. It's amazing what other people see as prized possessions.
- ▶ Car valeting.
- ▶ Cook a meal and charge students to come.
- ▶ Dog walking or dog sitting (less hassle than kids).
- ▶ Use the skills you have and tutor.
- ▶ Variation: tutor by Skype.
- ▶ Skill exchange: 'I give cookery classes in exchange for guitar lessons', Dundee student.
- ▶ Run errands.
- ▶ Gardening.
- ▶ Wedding photography: £250. No processing, no copyright, just give them the CD.
- ▶ Studying abroad: you have the international lingua franca at your fingertips – teaching/talk for money.

Turning your hobby into a money earner: Robert's story

Robert, a fourth-year history student at Dundee University, turned his guitar-playing hobby into a money spinner. He says, 'I usually charge £15–£20 an hour for lessons depending on the distance I have to travel. For gigs it can vary between £50 for a pub or club performance to over £100 for a wedding or function.

'Finding guitar pupils is easy as I worked for years in a guitar shop, and still know guys in those circles. I've had posters and business cards printed and have some material online – videos and solo recordings.

'My guitar playing is primarily a hobby and a passion. Being able to make money from it to facilitate my studies has made it all the more rewarding.'

University job shops

Now an essential part of university life, university job shops can be found on most campuses. Though similar, they have their own individual operating system but have one aim in common: to find students work.

Many jobs come from within the university itself. Pay for listed jobs is never less than minimum wage, often considerably more, and university job shops are increasingly popular with local employers. New jobs tend to arrive daily. Dundee University reckons around 300–500 jobs are registered a week.

Does your university have a job shop?

Check it out as soon as you arrive at university. Jobs go very quickly. Most students want or need to take jobs during the long summer vacations. Your university job shop or that of a university closer to home may be able to help you there.

i **where to look for jobs**
- University job shop
- Employment agencies
- Job centres
- Local employers on spec
- Local newspaper job ads
- *Summer Jobs Worldwide* by Susan Griffith, published by Vacation Work, includes over 50,000 jobs worldwide and is updated annually; website: www.crimsonbooks.co.uk

How Jason cuts his debt

'I'm a waiter/cook at the weekends working eight hours for the minimum wage.' As he is 18 that's the lower rate of £4.98 (£39.84 a week). 'Speaking to strangers and making them feel at home and cared for has helped me create a better persona when teaching.'

First year, Technology and Design with Education, Stranmillis University College

Jason's annual budget

Living: £1,620
Job: £1,147.32
Deficit: £472.68

Work experience and internships

For students, work experience offers the opportunity to gain specific experience of working in an area that will help them with their degree studies or entrance into a career. And if the placement is paid, then finding a placement during the vacations can be doubly beneficial.

People also talk about internships but this is essentially work experience by a different name. The word 'internship' came from the US and was spread throughout Europe by multinational companies, where it is now widely used. Sometimes the phrase 'vacation placement' is used.

Internships can be anything from six to 12 weeks during the summer to a full year's industrial placement. Some companies offer internships that start at any time throughout the year. Pay is usually given, but some companies offer expenses and experience only. Check what you are being offered.

Internships/work experience can lead to sponsorship for your next year of study, more work experience, and possibly a job offer (see Chapter 5 for more on sponsorship).

Weigh up what you are being offered, such as the company's reputation, opportunity for CV enhancement, money, experience, prospects, enjoyment and then decide: is this the right opportunity for me?

Pay during work experience as part of a sponsorship or internship is often, but not always, based on a salary of around £15,000–£18,000 per annum. So an eight-week placement could earn you approximately £2,500–£3,000.

> ### *i* advice note
>
> Don't leave it too late! If you want to work over the Christmas holidays, start planning early, even before you go to university – competition is high.

Internships after you graduate

In the current difficult job market some graduates are taking internships with companies as a lever to get into a company, to get experience and skills, and to enhance their CV. This hasn't helped the supply of summer internships available to undergraduates, which is another reason to start your search early.

Where to find work experience/internships

Organisations unable to offer sponsorship or industrial placements do offer vacation work experience and may even offer placements abroad. Try banks, insurance companies, accountancy and law firms, for example. Big companies such as BP, Shell, Credit Suisse, Barclays, Microsoft, National Grid, Exxon Mobil are also worth approaching (see below for more information).

The National Council for Work Experience (NCWE) holds an annual competition to find the company offering the best work placements. Winners past and present are always a good bet. Check out NCWE Awards at www.work-experience.org (see below for more information).

Companies may advertise in your university careers advice centre and in your university department. Your university may well have a list of possible opportunities.

Who to contact for work experience

- ▶ Local employers
- ▶ Local employment agencies
- ▶ Major employers
- ▶ Course directors
- ▶ College noticeboards
- ▶ Your university careers advisers
- ▶ University job shops
- ▶ The web
- ▶ Step (see page 186)

Big employers

Large companies such as **Procter & Gamble** offer what they call summer internships to students on a worldwide scale. They see it as a fair means of assessing students' ability and hope eventually to recruit most of their graduates through this scheme.

Centrica have been offering a 10-week summer placement programme to students in their penultimate year. Perks are £14,000 salary pro rata, free accommodation and experience in a range of areas. You earn: £2,692 plus free accommodation for 10 weeks' work.

i advice note

Check out the National Work Placement Exhibitions held generally in October – see www.work-placement.co.uk.

Don't forget the small employers

Small companies can be contacted direct. The advantage is that you could be the only intern and receive a great deal of attention and responsibility. Conversely, they may not know how to provide a good experience. It would then be up to you to make sure it worked.

The Shell Step programme

The Shell Step programme is an excellent route to work experience in smaller companies. This UK-wide scheme is designed to encourage small and medium-sized employers to take on undergraduates. Now in its 13th year, the programme offers 'project based' work experience lasting eight to 12 weeks over the summer vacation. Opportunities are open to second- and penultimate-year undergraduates of any degree discipline but focussing largely on science, technology and engineering students. A training allowance of around £210 per week is paid.

Money, and reducing your debt, is important, but finding the right job at the end of your degree course is even more vital. The competition out there is strong and getting stronger all the time, even for top graduates, so you need to make your CV stand out. Taking part in a 'Step' work placement in an area relevant to your future career aspirations is certainly one way to achieve this. There is a competition element related to the placement, and the achievements of students are assessed. A Step winner definitely has a CV advantage.

Step now also finds placements for students looking for a year-long sandwich placement (Step into Industry). For details, visit the Step website: www.step.org.uk, where you'll find more information, a database of current opportunities and an online application form for the summer programme. Alternatively contact your university's careers advisory service.

i **advice note**

Around half a million students look for work placements for the summer vacations. Competition is fierce. To avoid disappointment, start looking as soon as you have your university place. Work experience is becoming an important deciding factor on a student's CV, and an important aid to financial survival. Check out your university job shop or the website www.prospects.ac.uk.

Surf the net

There are a number of websites that can help you find work experience. Here are just a few of the best.

The graduate careers website Prospects: **www.prospects.ac.uk** has a work experience section.

The National Council for Work Experience (NCWE): **www. work-experience.org**, aims to support and develop quality work experience and encourage employers to offer more opportunities.

For the best part-time jobs try: **www.hotrecruit.com**, or you could go through UCAS: **http://yougo.co.uk**.

Other good websites for student jobs are: **www.justjobs4students. co.uk, www.student-part-time-jobs.com** and **www.activate. co.uk**.

Finally, try Target Jobs: **www.targetjobs.co.uk**.

Job check

Always keep your future career in mind when you head for holiday and even term-time jobs – that's the advice of the NCWE. Skills learnt from time spent working can make a great contribution to your CV and help convince a future employer that you are better than the competition. Whatever and wherever the job – supermarket, pub, the students' union – make the most of the opportunity to enhance your employability.

Interview advice: be prepared!

Expect a fairly intensive interview, as many companies think vacation work might lead to a more lasting relationship, e.g. full-time employment after you graduate, and are looking at you with this in mind. Because of that, it can be very competitive.

'Dress for success' is the advice to job-seeking students from Prospects. Whether attending an interview, recruitment fair or assessment day, creating a favourable impression is important. Getting the right look shows you understand the employer's business.

Industrial placements

The idea of the four-year sandwich course that includes an industrial placement was never envisaged as a financial life-saver, but many students find that a year in industry with a good salary helps them to clear their debts while they gain invaluable experience.

There are essentially two sorts of sandwich courses: those where you take a year out – usually the third year – to work in industry, and courses in which you alternate six months at university with six months at work.

With a full year out your university tuition fees will be cut to 50% or less. With the other type of sandwich course you may well find you have to pay full fees.

In the beginning, industrial placements were mainly for courses in engineering, but increasingly courses in business studies, retail, computer sciences and languages include an industrial placement year. Aberystwyth has taken this a step further with its YES – Year in Employment Scheme.

YES at Aberystwyth

The scheme offers students of any discipline the opportunity to undertake a year's paid work experience between the second and final years of their course. It's voluntary, so there's no pressure to do it, but it does give students a chance to 'test the water' before making a final career decision. The placement may be close to what you want to do, or something completely different. The percentage of YES graduates in employment six months after graduation is higher than amongst non-YES students.

Full details are available from the careers service at Aberystwyth University, email: careers@aber.ac.uk.

When is the best time to do a year in industry?

If you take your year in industry at 21 you are going to earn substantially more than you would at 18, so it could help pay off your debts. You will also know more about your subject so the experience can be more valuable. But if you take a year out before you start at university, the money you save will help to ease your finances once you start managing on student funding, and the experience will help with your studies.

If your industrial placement is taken as a gap year either before or after university you won't have to pay any fees.

The Year in Industry: work, earn, win, get ahead

If you are looking for paid work experience in industry, which could really help your future career and possibly lead to university sponsorship, the Year in Industry (YINI) are the people to contact. YINI is a nationwide programme run by the education charity EDT. Working with internationally renowned companies, YINI offers work placements that are challenging, rewarding and deliver real business experience to help you stand out from the crowd.

A work placement with YINI will:

- ▶ give your CV the competitive edge
- ▶ let you try out your degree or career choice
- ▶ give you 'real work' experience
- ▶ pay while you learn
- ▶ help you make the most of university
- ▶ help set you up for life with contacts, experience and opportunities.

In some instances, placement companies have gone on to sponsor YINI participants through university, and even offered them jobs at the end of their degree. YINI partners range from leading FTSE 100 companies to small innovative start-ups. Placements are for students interested in all areas of engineering, science, IT, e-commerce, business, marketing, finance and logistics.

Early applications are advised: YINI National Office, University of Southampton, Hampshire SO17 1BJ, tel: 023 8059 7061, email: info@yini.org.uk or website: www.etrust.org.uk.

An administration fee of £25 is payable after application and acceptance onto the scheme.

Who to ask about placements

Your university
If you are not a sponsored student, contact your university careers service or your faculty. It will have a list of possible employers who might offer placements. Contact employers directly – don't forget the smaller companies, which might have just one placement but choose not to advertise in case they get deluged.

Search the internet
Feed 'internship' into your favourite search engine. Also try www.monster.co.uk and www.gumtree.com/part-time-jobs.

A gap year to raise money

Most people think of a gap year as a way to travel the world and encounter new experiences, but if your aim is to save money, your best bet is to work as close to home as possible, where bed and board are likely to be at a very advantageous rate – if not free – and to avoid travel costs. In the past there were always plenty of jobs going in shops, restaurants and pubs, and you might still be lucky. Go for chains, such as Next, Tesco or a pub chain. You may then be able to get a transfer to a branch in your university town.

Since you have a whole year to work and a clutch of A levels to offer, you might be able to find a job with better pay and which stretches your ability more. But be realistic: you are not going to earn bags of gold. A gap-year student could expect to earn at least the minimum wage, which is £4.98 per hour for 18–20 year olds and £6.19 per hour for those aged 21 or above. Of the students who contacted us, fewer than half managed to save anything towards their university course, spending most of their earnings on travel. Though a gap year isn't only about earning money (many students see it as a chance to gain useful experience towards their career, to develop skills or to help others), having a wodge of money in the bank when you start university does help.

What students did in their gap years

Lydia worked for the Royal Bank of Scotland and gained wide experience, made some useful contacts and earned £5,000 before starting a degree in Economics at UWE. But she blew most of her earnings travelling to Hong Kong, Australia, New Zealand and South Africa.

Rachel didn't feel ready for university or leaving home, so she worked in her local library and her old school's library, earning £7,000. She managed to save £3,500 so had no serious money worries when she started her course in Pharmacology at Aberdeen.

Christopher worked in a sausage shop, where he learned how to mix up a 'mean banger'. It paid for his driving lessons, got him his wheels and gave him a £2,000 bank balance when he started a course in Business Administration at the UWE.

☑ where to look for gap year jobs

- ► On the internet: you will find gap year jobs, ideas, travel programmes, in fact every aspect of a gap year is covered.
- ► There are plenty of books out there to help you plan: type 'gap year' into the search box on Amazon and see what comes up.
- ► Try your local employers/newspapers for ads.

Last ditch!

You've tried all the traditional routes to find a job and some wacky ones as well no doubt, but it's come to nought. Don't give up! You are a student for heaven's sake, with a head full of ideas (hopefully). Start thinking outside the Job Centre box or even the university job shop. Be original (but legal), I mean, who wants to stack shelves anyway?

8 If you need a loan

You've looked at, and possibly tried, many of the money-raising options outlined in this book: grants, bursaries, sponsorship, part-time work, work experience, internships, the bank of mum and dad, study abroad, but the figures just don't stack up. There is still a big black hole in your finances.

When all else fails, the best and probably the only option left is a loan – possibly even two. But not any loans, we are talking about loans provided by the government. In this chapter we look at:

- ▶ how you get student loans
- ▶ what you are entitled to
- ▶ the likely debt sentence
- ▶ the interest you accumulate
- ▶ paying them off
- ▶ living with a loan
- ▶ personal loans
- ▶ loans to avoid.

A student loan is not like a mortgage or any other debt. If life takes a downward turn and you lose your job or never earn very much, unlike your house, your degree won't be repossessed, and you won't have the bailiffs knocking on the door. The debt just waits, goes into sleep mode, until life picks up and you can afford to pay it off again.

Graduates often marry graduates: but debts are not shared. Your debt is yours not your partner's. If one of you stays at home to look after the children, the debt lies dormant until they return to work. And if you never return to work it dies with you (well actually after 30 years) no matter how much your partner earns.

Having a debt of any size, but especially one around £50,000–£70,000 isn't an ideal situation to be in when starting your working life, but remember by the time you get round to paying it off, you should have a good degree in your pocket and potential earning power. Realistically, most students in the UK will end up with a loan. The main objective is to reduce it to the barest minimum.

So here's few facts to get straight about student loans.

1. You don't need cash to go to university, and that is true whatever the length of your course because there's no money to pay up front.

2. You will never have the debt collector thumping on your door demanding payment if you are out of work, providing, that is, your loans are 'student loans' from the government.

3. Loan repayments depend on how much you earn. In other words, how much you can realistically afford to pay, not the size of the debt.

4. If you never earn over £21,000 or enough to pay the loan off in full, it will be wiped out after 30 years. (This does not apply to students in Scotland where the repayment threshold is £15,795.)

So if you've tried everything else, student loans are the safest, least painful, and probably cheapest way to pay your way through university.

If you live in the UK you will be eligible for a loan, possibly two. How much you can get will depend on a number of factors:

▶ where you live
▶ where you study
▶ cost of your course
▶ family income
▶ grants received
▶ bursaries given
▶ university fee waivers
▶ your needs.

There are two loans on offer – tuition fee loans and maintenance loans. (For information on the non-repayable maintenance grant, see page 82.)

Tuition fee loans

The facts:

► higher education students can take out a loan to cover their fees

► the loan will be paid directly to your university. You will not see the money

► how much you are eligible for will depend on the amount of your fees

► the maximum fee loan is £9,000 per annum

► a fee loan is not means-tested

► EU students and part-time students in England can apply for a fee loan, but not a maintenance loan.

Reasons why you won't receive the maximum £9,000 per annum.

► The fees at your university are less than £9,000 per annum.

► You receive a bursary from your university which includes a fee waiver.

► Your family will be paying part of your fees.

► You live in Wales and the Welsh government will be paying towards your fees. The maximum fee loan in Wales is £3,465 per annum.

► You live and study in Scotland so there are no fees to pay and so no loan available. (Scottish students studying in England will pay fees and will be eligible for a fee loan.)

► You live and are studying in Northern Ireland. The maximum fee loan in Northern Ireland is £3,465 per annum, the rest of the fees are paid by the Northern Ireland government.

► You are a part-time student: you are eligible for a loan up to £6,750 per annum depending on intensity of course (note that the fee loan is not available to part-time students in the devolved regions).

► If you are on a course at an approved private university/college, the maximum loan available is £6,000 for full-time study, £4,500 for part-time study.

Is a fee loan a good idea?

The plus points of a fee loan are that the fees are always paid on time, so you don't need to worry about this while studying. Your debt remains under control, and there is no risk of you being barred from university because fees haven't been paid. Also, the payback is geared to your ability to pay.

> *i* **advice note**
>
> Should I take my university bursary (NSP) as a fee waiver, accommodation discount or cash? Received wisdom says go for the cash where possible. But we say, if you are cash rich, keep the debt down.

Debt is a worrying thought. And most sensible people would try to avoid it if possible. But going to university should not be a constant struggle for you or your parents. Study the payback arrangements featured on page 221. Taking out a mortgage on a house is seen as a good idea, why not taking out a mortgage for your future success and happiness?

Are fee loans available for all courses?

There are courses for which fee loans are not available, such as school-level courses (e.g. A levels or Scottish Highers, BTEC and SCOTVEC National Awards and City & Guilds courses for those over 19), postgraduate courses (except teacher training) and some correspondence courses.

Getting your fee loan

You apply for all funding at the same time. This includes bursaries, grants, fee loans and maintenance loans, if you need them at the start of your course. Fee loans are paid direct to your university. See pages 86–87 for full details on applying for funding and student finance, or visit the following websites:

- ▶ England: www.direct.gov.uk/sfvideos
- ▶ Wales: www.studentfinancewales.co.uk

- Northern Ireland: www.studentfinanceni.co.uk
- Scotland: www.saas.gov.uk.

I am from outside the UK, do I qualify for a fee loan?

Students from another EU country can apply for a loan to cover the cost of tuition fees, they should apply to the country in the UK where they intend to study (see details below). Help may also be available to migrant workers from an EEA country (European Economic Area), Switzerland, or the child of a Turkish migrant worker.

I cannot get a fee loan. What options do I have?

1. Talk to your local authority.
2. Talk to the institution where you want to take the course.
3. Apply for a professional and career development loan – see page 220.
4. Apply to professional bodies, trusts, foundations, benevolent funds – see Chapter 4.

Student maintenance loans

The student maintenance loan is quite different from the fee loan. For many students it is their main source of income. It is:

- cash in the bank
- partly means-tested
- intended to cover lodgings, food, books, pocket money, travel, socialising – but not fees.

The maintenance grant (see Chapter 4) is given to students from low-income families and does not have to be paid back. The maintenance loan does have to be repaid. The more maintenance grant you receive the less loan you can apply for.

Who is eligible

UK students who undertake full-time first degree or diploma of higher education courses at universities or higher education colleges are eligible for student maintenance loans. While there is no age limit on students taking out a fee loan, maintenance loans are only available to students aged under 60.

> ### ! It's a Fact
>
> Overseas students cannot apply for a maintenance loan. Even students from the EU who are classified as 'home' students for fee loans are not entitled to apply for a maintenance loan.

Amount of loan you can borrow

The amount that you can borrow is limited, and how much you receive is dependent on where you are studying and where in the UK you are domiciled. You don't have to take out the full amount, you can just take out however much you want, up to the maximum for which you are eligible that year. If you do not apply for the full amount at the start of the academic year, you can apply for the rest later that same year. It cannot be rolled over into the next year.

The maintenance loan is reviewed annually and usually increased. The loan will be paid termly, in three instalments depending on when you apply for it. Most students apply for funding online: see page 85 for more details on how to apply for funding, or visit the Student Finance website for your home country. Scottish students can visit the Student Awards Agency for Scotland at www.saas.gov.uk.

A portion of the loan is means-tested according to family income and not everybody can take out the full maintenance loan. For low-income families, part of the maintenance grant (see page 82) is paid in lieu of part of the maintenance loan, so those receiving the full or a large proportion of the full grant may find they are not entitled to the full loan. (See the example in Table 8.3.) It is hoped that any part of the means-tested loan you do not receive will be paid by your parents or spouse but this is not mandatory.

Independent students

Parents do not have to contribute if you are classed as an independent student. In other words, if you are:

- 25 or over
- married
- have been supporting yourself for three years.

If you are just living on student funding and your wits you should qualify for all the grants and bursaries going.

Family contribution

It is up to your family if and how they pay their contribution, and it may not be cash in the bank. Students told *Cut the Cost of Uni* that their parents:

- pay for accommodation
- pay bills: books, utilities, phone
- allow you to live at home for free
- maintain your car
- stock up your fridge
- give cash and let you budget
- wait till you ask.

! It's a Fact

Cut the Cost of Uni's research showed that . . .
72.3% of parents made a contribution
Average parental contribution: £1,008 per term

How the family contribution is assessed

All students in England will be able to receive 65% of the maximum student loan for maintenance and 75% in Wales and Northern Ireland (for Scotland see page 208). Where the student is not receiving a grant, the rest of the loan will be assessed on family income after certain allowances have been deducted. These allowances include pension and additional voluntary contributions, number of dependent children in the family and whether the parent is also a student.

If the residual (remaining) income is below the threshold then no family contribution is expected. Above that figure parents are expected to chip in but it is not compulsory. This is explained in more detail in Table 8.1.

Here's what some of our students had to say.

'It is unfair to judge the financial status of a student on the parents' income, since it's the student who will be paying off the debt.'

'It's the middle-class students that are suffering, with no grants and parents who can't afford to sub them.'

Note to parents

No parent is expected to contribute an amount that is more than the maximum means-tested portion of the loan for each student, however high their income – but many do as we have already stated in the book and as the budgets in this book reflect.

So how much do parents end up paying? The comparison table on the next page may help.

Table 8.1. Parental contributions across the UK

Support from parents per year	Region	Household income	Household assessed contribution
Parents start paying	England	£42,875	Nil *
	Wales	£50,020	Nil
	Northern Ireland	£41,540	Nil**
	Scotland	£24,276	£45
England: max contribution for one child	Live at home	£58,195	£1,532
	Study elsewhere	£62,125	£1,925
	Study in London	£69,745	£2,687
Wales: max contribution for one child	Live at home	£50,021+	Up to £75
	Study elsewhere	£57,000	£1,186
Northern Ireland: max contribution for one child	Live at home	£50,541	£938
	Study elsewhere	£53,035	£1,210
	Study in London	£57,643	£1,695
Scotland: max contribution for one child living and studying in Scotland	Live at home	£57,000 approx.	£3,965
	Study elsewhere	£61,000 approx.	£4,630

* Assessed contribution £1 for every £10 of total income over £42,875 until 65% of full maintenance loan remains.
** Assessed contribution £1 for every £9.50 of total income over £41,540 until 75% of full maintenance loan remains.

The portion of the maintenance loan that is means-tested in each region:

▶ 25% in Wales and Northern Ireland

▶ 35% in England

▶ a massive 85% in Scotland.

The four regions in the UK offer a slightly different funding package, which we'll discuss below.

The maintenance loan in England

If you receive a maintenance grant, the amount of loan for which you are eligible will be reduced by 50p for every £1 of grant. This means that if you receive the full grant, and if you qualify for a maintenance loan, your loan entitlement will be reduced by £1,625. Therefore, if you come from a lower-income household, you will have a smaller loan to repay.

All students will be able to receive 65% of the maximum student loan for maintenance. For students who do not receive a grant, the other 35% of the loan entitlement will be assessed on family income over £42,875 with your parents expected to contribute an additional £1 for every £10 earned over the threshold amount. As you can see, students from better-off families are highly dependent on parents making their contribution.

University bursaries through NSP are not included in calculations for maintenance loans.

Table 8.2. Full maintenance loan rates (England 2012–13)

		Full year maximum available
Students living away from their parents' home	In London	£7,675
	Elsewhere	£5,500
Students living in their parents' home		£4,375
Studying overseas		£6,535

Let's see how this relates to a real student budget.

Table 8.3. What university costs: Samantha's student budget showing annual income

Outgoings	Per term	Per year	Income per year	
Accommodation	£780	£2,340	Maintenance loan	£3,564
Food	£220	£660	Parents	£2,520
Socialising	£400	£1,200	Overdraft	£200
Gym	£45	£135	Sub-total	£6,284
Clothes	£100	£300		
Utilities	£60	£180		
Books/stationery	£100	£300		
Cigarettes	£144	£432		
Travel term	£130	£390		
Travel home	£40	£120		
Fees		£3,290	Fees loan	£3,290
Total		£9,347		£9,574

Samantha, second year, Psychology, Leeds; living in rented accommodation; anticipates her final debt will be about £27,000.

Parental contribution: special circumstances in England

Divorced parents
If your parents are divorced/separated, Student Finance will decide which parent they consider you are living with and assess their income, ignoring the income of the other parent.

Step-parents
If you have a step-parent or there is a cohabiting partner in the family where you live, then their income will be taken into account. However, maintenance received from an absent parent will not be considered as part of the household income when assessing income.

Parents made redundant
If the family income suddenly drops, for example because of redundancy, then contact Student Finance immediately. You could be entitled to a maintenance grant and more maintenance loan. Go to your online account and log in to the change of circumstances section. You should also tell your university, since many bursaries are linked to the amount of maintenance grant received.

What happens if my parents are not prepared to divulge their income?

You will not be assessed for a maintenance grant and will only be eligible for the non-means-tested portion of the maintenance loan.

If your parents cannot or will not make a contribution there is no way that parents can be made to pay their contribution towards your maintenance.

Does the parental contribution ever change?

Generally, the threshold at which parents begin to contribute towards maintenance is raised each year as the loan is increased. But not always.

Maintenance loans and additional funding for students in Wales

Table 8.4. Maintenance loans for Welsh students

	Money available
Away from home and studying in London	Up to £6,648
Away from home and studying elsewhere	Up to £4,745
Living in parental home	Up to £3,673
Studying abroad	Up to £5,770
Fee loan Wales	£3,465
Full Assembly Learning Grant in Wales	£5,000 – given where family income is £18,370 or below

Families with an income over £50,021 would be assessed for a contribution towards the student's maintenance. Twenty-five per cent of the loan is means-tested in Wales.

Table 8.5. Maintenance grants and loans for Welsh students

Household income	Assembly Learning Grant	Maintenance loan living away from home £4,745 maximum	Maintenance loan living in London £6,648 maximum	Maintenance loan living at home £3,673 maximum
£18,370	£5,000	£1,901	£3,804	£829
£25,000	£3,242	£2,800	£4,703	£1,728
£30,000	£2,033	£3,526	£5,429	£2,454
£34,000	£1,106	£4,082	£5,985	£3,010
£40,000	£711	£4,319	£6,222	£3,242
£45,000	£381	£4,517	£6,420	£3,445
£50,020	£50	£4,715	£6,618	£3,643

Let's see how this relates to a real student budget.

Table 8.6. What university costs: Aled's student budget showing annual income

Outgoings	per term	per year	Income per year	
Accommodation/ food (living at home)	£0	£0	Parents	£600
Snacks	£120	£360	Overdraft	£1,000
Socialising	£360	£1,080	Job	£6,000
Football/gym	£90	£270	Sub-total	£7,600
Mobile	£60	£180		
Travel petrol	£420	£1,260		
Car expenses	£480 approx.	£1,440		
Parking at university	£49.20	£147.60		
Fees		£1,400	Fee loan	£1,400
Total		£6,137.60		£9,000

Aled, third year, Sport Management, University of Glamorgan; living at home; anticipates his final debt will be about £12,000.

Covering your debt in Wales

Debt with fees: £11,965
Grant: –£5,000
Fee loan: –£3,465
Maintenance loan: –£3,804 (low because receiving full grant)
Black hole: £00.00

Maintenance loans in Northern Ireland

Table 8.7. Maintenance grants and loans for Northern Ireland students

	Money available
Maintenance grant	£3,475 maximum
Studying in Northern Ireland	£3,750
Studying in London	£6,780
Studying elsewhere in UK	£4,840
Studying in Republic of Ireland	£4,840

Twenty-five per cent of the loan is means-tested in Northern Ireland.

The full maintenance grant in Northern Ireland of £3,475 is given where family income is £19,203 or below. If the family income is over £41,540 no grant is given and income would be assessed for family contribution.

Table 8.8. Northern Ireland: maintenance grants and loans

Household income	Maintenance grant	Maintenance loan living away from home £4,840 maximum	Maintenance loan living in London £6,780 maximum	Maintenance loan living at home £3,750 maximum
£19,203	£3,475	£2,953	£4,893	£1,863
£25,000	£2,201	£3,289	£5,229	£2,199
£30,000	£1,215	£3,625	£5,565	£2,535
£35,000	£689	£4,151	£6,091	£3,061
£41,540	£0	£4,840	£6,780	£3,750

Maximum parental contribution in Northern Ireland

If they are earning £41,540 or below parents are not expected to contribute toward a student's maintenance. Above that figure and assessed family contribution will gradually increase to the maximum figures shown in Table 8.9 below.

Table 8.9. Maximum assessed parental contribution in Northern Ireland

Where living	Household income	Maximum assessed parental contribution
Full rate maintenance loan wherever you live/study	£41,540	Nil
Living at home	£50,541	£938
Living away from home	£53,643	£1,210
Living in London	£57,643	£1,695

Let's see how this relates to a real student budget.

Table 8.10. What university costs: Rachel's student budget showing annual income

Outgoings	Per term	Per year	Income per year	
Accommodation	£1,330	£2,660	Maintenance loan	£3,000
Food	£120	£360	Grant	£2,000
Socialising	£120	£360	Bursary	£1,100
Mobile phone	£120	£360	Dad phone	£360
Clothes	£90	£270	Mum	£1,050
Petrol	£360	£1,080	Job, piano teacher £40 pw	£1,440
Fees		£3,375	Fee loan	£0
Total		£8,870		£8,950

Rachel, first year, BEd Primary Education, Stranmillis University College, Belfast; living in fully catered halls; she anticipates her final debt will be about £14,000.

Covering your debt: living and studying in Northern Ireland

Debt with fees: £11,965
Grant: −£3,475
Fee loan: −£3,465
Maintenance loan: −£2,953 (figure is low because student is receiving full grant)
Black hole: £2,072

The maintenance loan in Scotland

Scotland operates a very different student funding scheme from the rest of the UK, though there are similarities.

All Scottish students studying in or outside Scotland can apply for a maintenance loan; and non-repayable bursaries (called grants in the rest of UK) are given to students from low-income families and replace part of the loan so as to reduce final debt. Higher income parents are expected to contribute more in Scotland than in the rest of the UK.

Table 8.11. Maintenance loans and additional funding available for Scottish students studying in Scotland (2012–13)

	Minimum	Maximum
Living in parental home	£620	£4,585 income assessed
Living elsewhere in Scotland (amount depends on family income and bursary; loan rates for final-year students are slightly lower)	£940	£5,570 income assessed
Non-repayable young students' bursary means-tested on family income up to £34,195		£2,640 income assessed
Additional means-tested bursary for independent students		£1,000 income assessed
Additional loans for students from low-income family where income is £22,789 or less		£810 income assessed

Approximately 85% of the loan is means-tested in Scotland.

Covering your debt: the maximum loan and bursary income p.a. in Scotland

Bursary: −£2,640
Maintenance loan: −£2,930
Possible extra loan: −£810
Total: £6,380
Anticipated debt: £8,500 per annum
Black hole: £2,120

Table 8.12. Maintenance loans and additional funding available for Scottish students studying outside Scotland (2012–13)

	Minimum	Maximum
Fee loan, not means-tested		£9,000
Bursary – income assessed, non-repayable. Independent students see note 3 below		£2,640 income assessed
Student maintenance loan living away from home and studying in London	£940	£6,690 income assessed
Studying elsewhere in UK	£940	£5,570 income assessed
Additional loan for students from low-income families		£810 income assessed

Notes on the maintenance loans in Scotland

1. Bursary given on family income up to £34,195.
2. Full bursary given where family income is £19,310 or less.
3. The maintenance loan is based on family income and bursary received.
4. Independent students can apply for an additional means-tested bursary of up to £1,000. They are not eligible for the young students' bursary.

Parental contribution in Scotland

Scotland has a different system of funding for students, and parents are expected to contribute more than parents in the rest of the UK and at a much earlier stage.

Table 8.13 below will give some idea of what Scottish parents could be facing. But remember, students in families where the residual income is up to £34,195 should be receiving an income-assessed young students' bursary. Families with a residual income below £24,275 (or £20,645 for spouses/partners) are not expected to contribute.

Table 8.13. Students' support package for Scottish students studying in Scotland

Income	Household contribution	Young students' bursary	Loan	Additional loan	Total
£18,000	£0	£2,640	£2,930	£810	£6,380
£20,000	£0	£2,518	£3,052	£503	£6,073
£23,000	£0	£1,986	£3,584	£0	£5,570
£26,000	£237	£1,453	£3,880	£0	£5,570
£29,000	£570	£921	£4,079	£0	£5,570
£32,000	£903	£389	£4,278	£0	£5,570
£35,000	£1,237	£0	£4,333	£0	£5,570
£38,000	£1,570	£0	£4,000	£0	£5,570
£44,000	£2,237	£0	£3,333	£0	£5,570
£50,000	£2,903	£0	£2,667	£0	£5,570
£56,000	£3,785	£0	£1,785	£0	£5,570
£62,000	£4,708	£0	£940	£0	£5,570

Note: income threshold is slightly lower for partners/spouses.
Source: www.saas.gov.uk

A deduction of £195 will be made from the assessed contribution for every dependent child other than the student. These figures are based on the full loan minus the minimum loan that a student can take out. If there is more than one child at university the maximum contribution a parent can be expected to make is £8,000 per annum, regardless of how many offspring they have at university or how much they earn. Although Scottish parents may look with envy at parents in the rest of the UK, who will be assessed to contribute considerably less than those in Scotland, English students will be accumulating a great deal more debt than their Scottish counterparts through fees.

Applying for funding in all regions of the UK

When and how to apply

If you want to receive your funding at the start of your course the application deadlines are likely to be May or June depending on your

Student Funding body. These are the same dates as those in applying for maintenance grants and tuition fee loans. See pages 86–87 for more information. Next year's deadlines are likely to be similar.

You can apply for a maintenance loan up to nine months after you have started your course. This is because students don't always know how much (if any) of the loan they are going to need. But if you want to have funding in place when you start your course, it's best to try and get your application in as early as possible.

There are three options for when to apply for a maintenance loan.

1. When you need it.
2. As late as possible: because you pay interest on the loan (see page 223).
3. As soon as possible. Some financially astute students take out their student loan even if they don't need it and invest it in a good interest-paying account with a bank or building society (not so easy to find in these credit crunch times). Make sure you know what you are doing. Check out interest rates first, and ensure you can get at your money quickly and easily if you are likely to need it – some high-interest rate accounts give limited access.

Covering your debt: with no help from family (London student)

Debt with fees: £17,500
Fee loan: –£9,000
Maintenance loan: –£4,988*
Black hole: £3,512
(*65% of maintenance loan. Shortfall because family won't divulge income or contribute)

When will my maintenance loan arrive?

Loan payments will be in three tranches, made at the beginning of each term directly into your bank account. If you receive a grant your loan will arrive at the same time. See page 97 for more detail. You can check the progress of your funding on your online account.

Panic! My loan and grant haven't arrived!

You are living in university accommodation

If you are living in university accommodation your university will probably be sympathetic if your cheque hasn't arrived and will wait until it does. But don't be too sure about this. Always tell your university if there's a hold-up. Some institutions will add a penalty to the bills of students who don't pay up on time.

If you run out of money and can't pay your bill at all, you will not be allowed to re-register for the next academic year. Worse still, if it's your final year, you will not get your degree until the bill is paid.

 cash crisis

As you won't receive your loan until you have arrived at your university or college, you will need to have some money of your own to get yourself there, and possibly to maintain yourself for several days until the cheque is cleared.

You are living in rented accommodation

Unfortunately, you can expect no leniency from your landlord. They expect to be paid on the dot, usually ask for rent in advance and may request an additional deposit. You will need funds to cover this.

Special circumstances

Second degree

You already have a degree and want to return to higher education – can you get financial support? The answer is unlikely. Any previous study is taken into consideration when making an assessment for student financial support. If you already hold an honours degree you do not usually qualify for any further support. There are some exceptions to this, such as medicine and dentistry, but you would need to discuss this with your university.

Changing course

If you change to another course in the same institution, your entitlement to a maintenance loan may well stay the same, but your fees could be different. If you transfer to another institution the fees may be different.

The major problem arises if you change to an institution or a course that does not attract student support or if there is a break in your studies before you join the new course.

If you transfer from one course to another or withdraw from your current course, it is very important that you not only discuss this with your institution but also talk to Student Finance in your region as soon as possible.

Study in private higher education institutions

Students attending an approved private HE institution that is designated for funding by the Department for Business, Innovation, and Skills (England) should be able to take out a loan to cover fees of up to £6,000 (£4,500 part time). This may not be enough to completely cover your fees as these can be higher than in other types of university. You may also be able to take out a maintenance loan and could be eligible for a maintenance grant. The course could cover any subject – theology and complementary medicine, for example.

Industrial placements

If you need to take a sandwich year during your course you may apply for a fee loan (see page 195) and also for a maintenance loan (see page 197). If you are on a full year's industrial training you will only be eligible for the reduced rate of loan, which is approximately half the full rate.

Longer courses

If your course is longer than 30 weeks you can claim for an extra loan, for each week you have to attend your course. This will be means-tested. If your course year is 45 weeks or longer, you will receive a loan based on 52 weeks.

i advice note

Postgraduates are not entitled to a student loan unless they are taking a PGCE course. So if as an undergraduate you do not need the loan or all of the loan now but are thinking of going on to do a postgraduate course, it might be worth your while taking out the student loan and investing it so the money is there to help you through your postgraduate studies later on. If you are not a financial whizz kid, take advice. The student loan is a really cheap way of borrowing money, but you don't want to build up debt unnecessarily.

Further information

Student Finance England helpline tel: 0845 300 5090 between 8a.m. and 8p.m. Monday to Friday and from 9a.m. to 5.30p.m. weekends for financial information, including information on your loans.

Braille and audio editions of Student Finance England information available at website: www.direct.gov.uk/studentfinance.

For students in Scotland: contact SAAS, Gyleview House, 3 Redheughs Rigg, South Gyle, Edinburgh EH12 9HH, tel: 3003 555 0505, email: saas.geu@scotland.gsi.gov.uk or website: www.saas.gov.uk.

For students in Northern Ireland: www.studentfinanceni.co.uk, Rathgael House, Balloo Road, Bangor, Co. Down BT19 7PR or tel: 0845 600 0662.

For students in Wales: National Assembly for Wales, Higher Education Division 2, 3rd floor, Cathays Park, Cardiff CF10 3NQ, tel: 0845 602 8845 8a.m.–8p.m. Monday to Friday, Saturday 9a.m.–1p.m., website: www.studentfinancewales.co.uk.

Banks, bank loans and overdrafts

Choosing a bank

You will need to set up a bank or building society account before you go to university. The Student Loans Company won't pay out your loan/grant unless you have an account. Most bank and building societies are keen to attract students' accounts because they see students as potential high-earners and long-term customers. Statistics show that you are more likely to change your partner than your bank. So making the right choice is important.

Even if you go for online banking, it is a good idea to choose a bank or building society that has a branch located close to your home or place of study. While you can use the cash machines in most branches of most banks and building societies, if you are struggling with debt it's important to be able to speak to someone face to face.

Many banks offer freebies to entice students to join them. Don't let these cloud your judgement. A USB stick isn't for life; a bank often is. One of the most important student offers is the **interest-free overdraft.**

Interest-free overdrafts for students

Important points to consider are the following.

- To get the interest-free overdraft facility you must tell your bank you are a student.
- If your overdraft goes over the set interest-free limit, you will be charged interest.
- You may be able to negotiate a larger interest-free overdraft, but don't rely on it.
- Use the bank's interest-free limit rather than building up debt on a credit card.
- All or part of your overdraft is wiped out when your funding (loan, grant, bursary) hits your bank account, so you may be short of cash to spend.
- A bank overdraft eventually has to be paid off.

An overdraft could add up to an extra £3,000 to your spending power. Do students use this facility? You bet they do! Our research showed that around 50% of students thought they would be overdrawn during their course. More debt it may be, but if you are struggling, don't turn your back on the interest-free overdraft facilities – they are considered by many students to be an essential part of their income, helping to fill that financial black hole between loan payments.

Interest-free overdrafts: more debt or a life-saver?

The answer is probably both. Most banks and some building societies will offer students overdraft facilities on special terms, usually including an interest-free overdraft facility of £1,000–£3,000.

Should you go for the larger or the smaller sum? The larger gives you more financial wriggle room, but the bigger the overdraft the bigger the temptation and the debt. It is a loan and eventually it has to be paid back.

An overdraft is intended mainly to help you during those difficult financial periods. For example:

► when your loan hasn't yet arrived

► when you've run out of cash at the end of the term

► to cover a temporary financial problem. It is better only to use the bank's interest-free facility if you are certain you will be able to pay the overdraft back once you graduate

► final-year students often ask for an overdraft, to buy new clothes for an interview

► most banks won't start charging interest on student overdrafts immediately after you graduate, giving you time to get a job. This can be several months, but check it out with your bank

► some banks offer students longer-term loans at competitive rates, which should be investigated with care.

In general though, banks are not the best bet for long-term borrowing for students – the student loans are, since the interest rate is low and payback terms are managed. See 'Student loans: paying them back' page 221.

Going over your overdraft limit

If you go over your overdraft limit, get on the phone to your bank immediately. Many of the leading banks have campus branches or at least a branch in the town geared to dealing with students. They'll probably be sympathetic and come up with a helpful solution.

Paying back your overdraft

Most banks will also offer special arrangements for paying the overdraft off once you graduate. Check out these arrangements before you step on the slippery slope to debt. Ask them:

► how long will they give me to pay it off?

► what will the charges be then?

► how long does the interest-free overdraft last?

These questions will help you to find the best arrangement for you – far better than falling for the freebies.

Always check details with individual banks. To compare try Moneymagpie: www.moneymagpie.com/article/best-banks-for-students.

What students say

'When my bank offered an interest-free overdraft I thought the £1,500 was mine to spend. Now I have to think about paying it back. Very distressing!'

'Don't borrow from a lot of places. If you've got an overdraft and a student loan, that's probably enough.'
                              First year, Urban Planning Studies, Sheffield.

---

i **advice note**

'I haven't got the money at the moment so I'll buy it on my credit card.'

Easily done, but be warned – although credit cards are fine as a payment card, if you don't pay off your bill by the end of the month you end up paying interest and accumulating more debt.

Can I open two student bank accounts with two different banks?

The banks don't like or encourage it, but the fact is you can and there is not much they can do about it. However, two overdrafts to pay off when you graduate is not recommended, especially if you have students loans as well.

☑ **loans to be avoided**

Avoid these types of loans at all costs:

- ▶ credit card debt
- ▶ payday loans
- ▶ loan sharks
- ▶ high risk loans.

With the loans mentioned the interest is high and they need to be paid back pretty smartly. A student overdraft will also have to be paid back once you graduate but most banks will give a student time to do so. Check out their special payback arrangements before you decide on a bank.

Personal loans

A personal loan is quite different from an overdraft. It is usually used when you want to borrow a much larger sum, over a longer period – say several years. It differs from an overdraft in that you borrow an agreed amount over a set period of time and the repayments are a fixed amount, generally monthly. You might take out a loan to pay for your course fees, but not for short-term credit to tide you over until your next grant cheque arrives.

> ### *i* advice note
>
> Don't fall into the hands of a loan shark. Any loan offered to students, except from a recognised student-friendly source e.g. banks, building societies, parents or the Student Loans Company, should be treated with the utmost caution and suspicion. It's bound to cost you an arm and a leg, and lead to trouble.

Professional and career development loans

Professional and career development loans are designed for people on vocational courses (full time, part time or distance learning) of up to two years where your fees aren't paid, and you can't get support from your employer or the government.

The loan is a bank loan. You take it out with a participating bank and can borrow between £300 and £10,000. Once you have completed your studies you then start paying it back in the normal way. The difference with this kind of loan is that the government (through the Skills Funding Agency) pays the interest on your loan while you are studying and for one month afterwards. You will then pay interest at the rate fixed when you took it out while also paying the loan off. The scheme is funded by a number of high-street banks (Barclays, the Co-operative and the Royal Bank of Scotland) and administered by the National Careers Service.

If the course you take lasts more than two years (or three years if it includes work experience), you may still be able to use a professional and career development loan to fund part of your course.

Shop around the different providers and compare the terms offered before making a choice. For full details, see: www.direct.gov.uk and search for 'career development loans' or phone 0800 100 900.

'Get a job – the student loan seems like a lot of money, but it doesn't cover even the essentials.'

Psychology, Hull

Student loans: paying them back

This is the painful bit – but it's not as painful as you would imagine, and though your loans may be larger than your predecessors', your monthly payback bills will be lower.

It may take a long time, but a system has been worked out that allows you to pay back what you borrowed in line with what you earn. Remember, the student loan is quite different from a mortgage or a bank loan. If you don't earn, you don't have to pay, it's as simple as that.

Student loans: the upside

If you are made redundant: you just stop repaying your debt – no threatening demands. It will accumulate interest until better times. Also, if you stop work to have a family there will be no further demands until you return to work.

Student loans: the downside

You pay interest on what you have borrowed, so the longer you take to pay off the debt the larger it grows.

If you marry an equally indebted student the burden can be doubled as you both have loans to pay off.

When and what do you pay

If you have a fee and a maintenance loan they are rolled into one debt. You repay nothing until the April after you have graduated, and then only when your income is over £21,000 per annum (£15,795 in Scotland). If your earnings are below that threshold, you pay nothing.

The amount you pay is related to your salary, so whether you have a loan of £1,000 or £60,000, your monthly repayments will be the same as long as you stay on the same salary. See Table 8.15 below for details of the interest you will be charged.

Table 8.14. Approximate loan repayment rates for the year 2012–13 for students in England, Wales, Northern Ireland

Annual income up to	Monthly repayments (approx.)	Monthly salary (approx.)
£21,000	£0	£1,750
£22,000	£7.50	£1,833
£24,000	£22	£2,000
£27,000	£45	£2,250
£30,000	£67	£2,500
£40,000	£142.50	£3,333
£50,000	£217.50	£4,166

In terms of repayments – you pay approximately 9% of your salary over £21,000.

Table 8.15. Approximate loan repayment rates for the year 2012–13 for students who live in Scotland

Annual income up to ...	Monthly repayments (approx.)
£15,795	£0
£16,000	£1
£21,000	£39
£25,000	£69
£30,000	£106.50
£40,000	£181.50
£50,000	£256.50
£60,000	£331.50

In terms of repayments – you pay 9% of salary over £15,795.

Repayments for part-time students will be the same as full-time students since they are based on ability to pay and not how much you owe. Check when you start paying back, as this could be before the end of your course if you are earning over £21,000.

Making repayments

Repayments will be collected through HM Revenue & Customs and will be deducted from your pay packet at source. Probably all you will know about it is an entry on your pay slip. The debt is written off after 30 years whatever the outstanding amount.

The rules about paying back your loan are reviewed every year to make sure graduates can realistically pay back what they owe.

Do you pay back more than you borrow?

YES! And now we are talking about even more money. The great boast of successive governments has been that the interest rates paid on loans was linked to inflation, so while the actual figure you paid would be higher, the value of the amount you paid back was broadly the same as the value of the amount you borrowed. Not any more! Student loans cost money.

This is how the new pay-back scheme works (not applicable in Scotland).

▶ While you are studying: interest will be charged at RPI rate of inflation + 3%

▶ After study and earning under £21,000: the interest charged will be RPI rate of inflation.

▶ After study and earning £21,000–£41,000: there is a gradual increase to maximum charge RPI inflation + 3%.

▶ After study, earning over £41,000: interest charged is RPI rate of inflation + 3%.

So what does this all add up to?

The only thing we can say for sure is we are talking about thousands rather than hundreds of pounds. Paying interest on your loans is not an exact science because:

- the RPI figure over the next 3–4 years is unknown but it is currently running at 3.6%
- fee increases are unknown but likely
- maintenance loan increases are unknown but there have always been increases each year.

The only certainty is that even before you start paying back your debt you will owe more than you borrowed.

Exceptions to paying back your loan

You will be expected to pay back your loan unless you fall into the following categories:

- you never earn more than £21,000 a year
- you become permanently disabled
- you die!

After 30 years any loan that is left unpaid will be written off no matter how much or how little of it is left.

Paying off your debt early

Yes, you are allowed to do it and there will be no penalty for doing so.

There was much talk when the new scheme was first announced that students who earned enough would be charged for paying off their debt early. This idea has been abandoned.

Is it a good idea to pay off your debts early?

Though one should be encouraged to pay off debts as soon as possible, many students will find they never actually pay off their debt in full, if any at all. It depends on what you expect to earn. Low earners should check out the 30 year debt wipe-out rule (listed above). It might be working in your favour.

Will I be able to get a mortgage?

Student loans do not show on your credit rating files, so would not be included in your ability to pay off a loan. If a lender asks for such details you should tell them. This new student loan repayment system is less onerous than for past students so is unlikely to have as much, if any, impact on your ability to take out and pay off a mortgage. Saving for a deposit might be more difficult.

'Student debt is bad enough, but the "invisible" debt is worse – overdrafts, credit cards, borrowing from family – all of which has to be paid back.'

Being able to pay your loan back

Although students are facing the possibility of graduating with a massive debt, and despite the news that graduates in 2012 are struggling to find jobs, starting salaries for graduates with good second-class honours degrees in a blue-chip company are on the increase. This year, 2012, starting salaries are expected to be around a median of £26,000, an increase of around 4% on last year. But the 50 dollar question is, are you going to be a success story? Or like many graduates, start work on a much lower salary.

Table 8.16. Where are the big graduate starting salaries to be earned?

Investment bank or fund managers	£39,000
Law firm	£35,500
Actuarial work	£28,500
Consulting	£27,750
IT	£26,000
Manufacturing engineering	£26,000
Sales/customer management/business development	£25,250
Accountancy	£25,000
General management	£25,000
Financial management	£25,000
Science	£25,000

Source: AGR Graduate Recruitment Survey 2012 – Winter Review (employers by career area)

The graduate market is currently very volatile with recruiters predicting a slight drop in vacancies, of around 1.2%, according to the *AGR Graduate Recruitment Survey 2012 – Winter Review*. So what it will be like in three or four years' time, when this year's first-year students graduate, is anyone's guess. But it's worth remembering that, if you can't find work, the SLC will wait for repayment; the banks, however, may not be so sympathetic, although most do offer special overdraft facilities to graduates, which you should investigate.

Employers paying off your loan

When the loan scheme first came in, many employers thought they might need to offer the 'carrot' of paying off students' loans if they wanted to attract the best graduates. Whether the government was hoping that employers would step in and clear students' debts in this way was a question often discussed in the national press. Two years ago around a quarter of AGR members reported offering golden hellos of £1,000 to £4,000 to attract the best graduates but this no longer seems to be so. With fees and debts now escalating it's something that many graduates would welcome.

Bankruptcy

Wherever you reside in the UK, declaring bankruptcy is not an option for students wanting to avoid paying back their student loan. In 2004 a loophole in the law was closed making the student loan impervious (non-provable) to bankruptcy. So even recent legislation to make going bankrupt easier won't help. The debt will still be there and still be yours.

Special circumstances for loans for EU and non-EU students

EU students
This does not include UK students.

▶ All EU students will be able to take out a fee loan to cover their fees and pay it off gradually once they graduate.

▶ EU students are not entitled to apply for a maintenance loan, and are unlikely to receive a maintenance bursary.

▶ EU students will not receive a maintenance grant.

Non-EU students

- ► You will not be eligible for a fee loan, a maintenance loan, grant or any help with funding.

- ► Some universities do give bursaries to overseas students and some charities have special funds for overseas students (see Chapter 4).

- ► Most universities and colleges do have a designated overseas adviser whom you could ask for help.

- ► Non-EU students wanting to gain work experience in this country after they graduate can stay up to two years.

Disabled students

- ► If you are severely disabled as an undergraduate you would still be eligible for a student loan whether you are likely to be able to pay it off or not.

- ► Any disability-related financial entitlements you receive will be disregarded when calculating your repayment amounts.

- ► Phone the SLC helpline free on 0845 607 7577.

Studying abroad as part of your degree course

You can get some extra financial help but it will be a loan. If you study abroad for at least 50% of an academic quarter (which normally means a term), then you are eligible for an overseas rate of loan, which for 2012–13 is £6,535 in England. The amount for other regions of the UK may differ slightly.

Last word on loans

We called loans the 'funding of last resort', and when you see the interest you have to pay we were probably right to do so. But if you do have to resort to them, and most students do, they are not going to blight your life. The student loan scheme has been organised so paying loans back will always leave you with a good income to live on. As one student told us, 'I never think about paying off my loans. It's just like paying an extra tax. Something you see on your payslip but you don't miss because you never had the money in the first place.'

Conclusion

We have looked at the many things you can do to reduce your university debt – from the major savings such as sponsorship, grants, bursaries, scholarships, a well-paid job, to the smaller options like ferreting out special offers, student reductions, sharing books and catering together. Once you start your course you may discover other ideas. If you do, let us know by emailing us at info@trotman.co.uk and we will include them in the next edition.

But whatever you do, don't let the thought of debt put you off.

University is still a great experience. Enjoy every minute of it wherever you study. Be concerned about money, but don't get stressed out. Most students do find a way of making the sums add up and in some very ingenious ways. Hopefully this book has shown you how. Best of luck!